Cambridge English
Preliminary for Schools
PRELIMINARY ENGLISH TEST FOR SCHOOLS PET

T0346293

CENGAGE
Learning·

Australia • Brazil • Japan • Korea • Mexico • Singapore • Spain • United Kingdom • United States

CENGAGE Learning®

Cambridge English Preliminary for Schools
Practice Tests
Teacher's Book

Publisher: Gavin McLean

Director of Content Development: Sarah Bideleux

Project Editor: Tom Relf

Production Controller: Elaine Willis

Art Director: Natasa Arsenidou

Text/cover Designer: Sofia Ioannidou

Compositor: Ken Vail Graphic Design

Acknowledgments

Thanks to signature manuscripts for their help with the production of this title

Edited by Liz Hammond

Audio produced by Liz Hammond.

Recorded at GFS-PRO Studio and Motivation Sound Studios. Mixed at GFS-PRO Studio by George Flamouridis.

ISBN: 978-1-4080-6153-4

National Geographic Learning
Cheriton House, North Way, Andover, Hampshire,
SP10 5BE United Kingdom

Cengage Learning is a leading provider of customized learning solutions with office locations around the globe, including Singapore, the United Kingdom, Australia, Mexico, Brazil and Japan. Locate our local office at **international.cengage.com/region**

Cengage Learning products are represented in Canada by Nelson Education Ltd.

Visit National Geographic Learning online at **ngl.cengage.com**
Visit our corporate website at **cengage.com**

Photo Credits

The publishers would like to thank shutterstock.com for permission to reprint the majority of photos in this book. Further acknowledgment goes to:
p. 157: Chad Ehlers/Alamy images (for photo of the Ice Hotel); **p. 185:** Shutterstock (for photo of the astronauts by vicspacewalker).

Illustrations

Kate Rochester c/o Pickled ink

Printed in the United Kingdom by Lightning Source
Print Number 03 Print Year 2017

Contents

Introduction

Cambridge English: PET for Schools Exam Overview

Cambridge English: Preliminary English Test for Schools is produced by University of Cambridge ESOL Examinations and is an internationally recognised exam for students at Level B1 of the Common European Framework of Reference for Languages.

The *PET for Schools* exam has three papers: Paper 1 Reading and Writing, Paper 2 Listening and Paper 3 Speaking.

Papers 1 and 2 are administered in one session. Paper 3 Speaking is administered in a separate session, usually on a different day, with two examiners and two candidates. The papers are structured as follows:

Paper 1 Reading and writing

Timing	Task	Task focus	Scoring
1 hour 30 minutes	**Reading Part 1** Five very short texts such as signs, emails and notices followed by five three-option multiple-choice questions	Reading real-world notices and other short texts for the main message	1 mark each
	Reading Part 2 Five items in the form of descriptions of people to match to eight short texts	Reading multiple texts for specific information and detail	1 mark each
	Reading Part 3 Ten true/false questions with a long text	Scanning for specific information	1 mark each
	Reading Part 4 One long text followed by five four-option multiple-choice questions.	Reading for detailed comprehension, gist, inference and global meaning; understanding attitude, opinion and writer purpose	1 mark each
	Reading Part 5 A factual or narrative gapped text followed by ten four-option multiple-choice questions.	Understanding grammar and vocabulary in a text	1 mark each
	Writing Part 1 Five sentence transformation questions on the same theme	Rephrasing and reformulating information using different structures	1 mark each
	Writing Part 2 A short communicative message such as an email or postcard based on a short prompt	Writing 35–45 words focusing on communicating three specific content points	Marks out of 5 (see below for marking criteria)
	Writing Part 3 A choice of an informal letter or a story	Writing about 100 words focusing on control and range of language	Marks out of 15 (see below for marking criteria)

Paper 2 Listening

Timing	Task	Task focus	Scoring
30 minutes approx. (each part is heard twice)	**Part 1** Seven short unrelated monologues or dialogues with seven three-option multiple-choice questions with visuals	Listening to identify key information from short exchanges	1 mark each
	Part 2 An interview or monologue with six three-option multiple-choice questions	Listening to identify specific information and detail	1 mark each
	Part 3 A monologue with six gaps to complete	Listening to identify, understand and interpret information	1 mark each
	Part 4 A dialogue with six true/false questions	Listening for detail, attitude and opinion	1 mark each

Paper 3 Speaking

Timing*	Task	Task focus	Scoring
2–3 minutes	**Part 1 Interview** A conversation between the examiner and each candidate (spoken questions)	Using social and interactive English to give basic personal information about past and present experiences and future plans	(see below for marking criteria)
2–3 minutes	**Part 2 Simulated situation** A conversation between the candidates using visual prompts	Using functional language to suggest, recommend, discuss alternatives and come to an agreement	(see below for marking criteria)
3 minutes	**Part 3 Long turn** Each candidate has a minute to talk about two related photographs	Describing photographs and managing discourse using appropriate vocabulary	(see below for marking criteria)
3 minutes	**Part 4 Discussion** A general conversation between the candidates developing the theme of Part 3	Talking about interests, opinions, experiences, etc	(see below for marking criteria)

* This assumes two examiners (one interlocutor who speaks with the candidates, and one who silently assesses) and two candidates. In cases where there are an uneven number of candidates at an exam centre, the final Speaking test of the session is taken by three candidates together, with a total time of thirteen to fifteen minutes rather than twelve.

Marking and scoring

Each skill is marked out of 25 so the total is 100. Each paper is graded A–E, with a C grade being satisfactory. However, it is not necessary to gain a satisfactory level in each part to get the 70% needed to pass the whole exam.

The standardised scores are given out of 100.
Pass with Merit = 85–100
Pass = 70–84

Candidates who do not pass PET but have demonstrated ability at the level below are awarded a certificate at level A2. Candidates below this level are awarded a failing grade.

Marking criteria for Writing

Each piece of writing is assessed with reference to two mark schemes: one based on the examiner's overall impression (The General Impression Mark Scheme), the other on the requirements of the particular task (The Task Specific Mark Scheme). A band from 0–5 is awarded depending on how well the candidate performs in terms of covering the content and communicating the message, achieving the desired effect on the target reader, range and accuracy of structure and vocabulary, organisation and use of linking devices.

Marking criteria for Speaking

The interlocutor awards an impression mark for Global Achievement.
The Assessor awards candidates a band from 0–5 depending on how well they perform over the whole test in terms of four criteria:
- Grammar and vocabulary – How accurate and appropriate is the candidate's range of grammatical forms and vocabulary?
- Discourse management – How well are the candidate's utterances linked to form coherent, relevant, logical speech? Can the candidate speak consistently using complete sentences?
- Pronunciation – How well does the candidate produce sounds and use stress and intonation to make what they say understandable?
- Interactive communication – How appropriately does the candidate initiate and respond to interaction? Can candidates sustain the interaction without too much hesitation?

Contents of the book

This book contains eight full practice tests for the *Cambridge English: Preliminary English Test for Schools*. There is also a section-by-section introduction to the test which explains what candidates need to do in each section and what the focus of each section is. The first three tests in the book also contain useful guidance and tips for candidates.

Guidance for candidates

These sections are designed to help you achieve the best possible results by giving you an overview of the different parts of the exam and what is expected from you in each one. There is valuable information on the exam format and length, type of questions and the skills that you need in order to do well.

Tips

These sections focus more closely on the types of questions you will face in each part of the exam. The tips break down the structure of individual questions and show you how the questions actually work. They show you what you need to look for and be careful of. They remind you of the most important things to think about in each part of the exam. They explain why certain answers are correct and why others may look right but are in fact wrong. You can use these tips to become familiar with each part of the exam and so complete the tasks with more confidence.

Glossary

There is a glossary at the back of the book giving definitions of some words and phrases you may not know, including phrasal verbs and idioms.
You will often find that you can answer a question even if you don't know the meaning of a particular word or phrase. Maybe you can guess the meaning from the context or the question may not require you to actually know the meaning. Try to answer the questions in these practice tests before you look up the meanings of any unknown items in the glossary.
The words and phrases in the glossary are in the order you will meet them in the book.

Audio CDs

The CDs that come with this book have recordings which are just like the ones in the actual test and give you valuable practice for the listening paper. Remember the listening paper has the same number of marks as the other three parts of the test.

Cambridge English: Preliminary English Test for Schools

The *Cambridge English: Preliminary English Test for Schools* tests the practical language skills you need when using English as an international system of communication for travel, work or study in an English-speaking environment. Each test covers all four language skills: listening, reading, writing and speaking, and you have to complete tasks which reflect real life.
The topics in the tests are selected to be interesting to you and the practice you will get will be useful to you even if you are not actually going to take the exam.
These practice tests with the guidance, tips and glossary sections will help you develop your confidence in English and be ready to show what you can do.

Practice Test 1

READING PART 1

Questions 1 – 5

Look at the text in each question.
What does it say?
Mark the correct letter **A**, **B** or **C**.

Example:

0

> Dear Lucy,
>
> Spain is great! It's so hot here and there are no clouds in sight! Much better than rainy England! I'm having lots of fun.
> See you back at school.
>
> Jack

What does Jack say?

A   The weather is good where he is.

B   England is nicer than Spain.

C   It is cloudy in Spain.

Answer: | 0 | A ▬ | B ☐ | C ☐ |

1

> Nick,
>
> I've gone to the supermarket. Do your maths homework and I'll check it when I get in. See you later.
>
> Mum

What should Nick do?

A   finish his homework before his mum gets home

B   meet his mum at the supermarket

C   check that he has maths homework to do

2

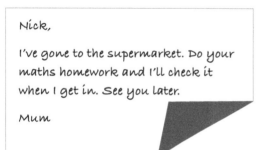

> 12:20 PM
> Hi Alice,
> I'm out shopping and I've seen that red skirt that you wanted. Shall I get it for you?
> Text me back.
> Holly

What does Holly want to know?

A   whether Alice wants to go shopping with her

B   whether Alice likes red clothes

C   whether Alice wants her to buy a skirt

3

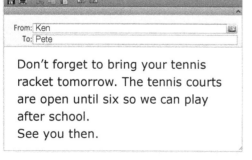

> From: Ken
> To: Pete
>
> Don't forget to bring your tennis racket tomorrow. The tennis courts are open until six so we can play after school.
> See you then.

Why has Ken written the email?

A   to tell Pete where they can play tennis

B   to remind Pete to bring his racket

C   to tell Pete when they should meet

4

Build your own model aeroplane!

Parts, glue and paint included.

Read instructions first.

Not suitable for children under 4.

The label says the aeroplane

A   is for people over a certain age.

B   is already painted and ready to use.

C   is one of a set of toy models.

5

KEEP OFF THE GRASS!

Please walk on the path around the park and keep dogs on leads.

Thank you.

A   Dogs aren't allowed in the park.

B   There are lots of paths in the park.

C   Visitors to the park shouldn't walk on the grass.

GUIDANCE FOR CANDIDATES

The Reading part of the test is combined with the Writing in one paper of 1 hour 30 minutes. No extra time is allowed for you to transfer your answers to the special answer sheet at the end of the test, so you should make sure you have enough time to do this. You should spend about 50 minutes on the Reading part of the paper.

The texts you will read are of different types selected and adapted from real-world pieces of writing in magazines, newspapers, websites, leaflets, brochures, short notes and emails. All the topics are chosen to be of general interest to eleven to fourteen year-olds.

Prepare for this part by reading a variety of short and longer text types. You're already reading texts in your course book, but try and read other things that interest you on the Internet in English and ask your teacher to bring in short texts, advertisements and notices for you to read in class or at home. If you have a hobby or interest in music, sport or celebrities, see if you can find an English language magazine or website similar to one you have in your own country. When you read something in English, don't spend too much time looking up words in a dictionary – try to guess the meaning and focus on getting the general idea of a text.

In the test itself, make sure you read the instructions to each part carefully. Parts 1 and 5 have examples to help you and the texts in parts 2, 3, 4 and 5 each have a title to give you an idea of what you are going to read about.

As you have about 50 minutes for the Reading part of Paper 1, you should spend no more than ten minutes on each of the five parts. When you do practice tests, time yourself and see which part usually takes you the longest to complete so you can give yourself a bit more time to do this part in the actual test.

Remember you can write anything you like to help you on the question papers – underline, cross out, make notes. However, your answers on the answer sheet must be clearly filled in with a pencil – not a pen.

Part 1 consists of five very short texts, such as signs, advertisements, notices, labels, messages, notes or emails. Each text is followed by a multiple-choice question with three options. Each correct answer gets one mark. This part tests reading and how well you can understand the main message of various short texts. There is only one correct answer.

Quickly read the text first before you read the question and options. Think about what kind of text it is. There may also be a picture which can help you decide if the text is an email, or a notice, or a poster. This will help you get a general idea of what it's about and where the text is from.

Now look carefully at the three options. Some items include an introductory question and some do not. Pay special attention to the introductory question if there is one. Compare each option with the text and decide which one is really the same as what the text says or means. If you're not sure of the answer, cross out the option or options that are obviously wrong first. This will leave you with fewer choices.

Underline in the text where you find the answers to questions. This will help you quickly check your answers at the end.

Answer all the questions, even if you aren't sure of an answer. You won't lose marks for incorrect answers.

READING `PART 2`

Questions 6 – 10

The teenagers below all want to take up a new hobby or other activity.
On the opposite page, there are descriptions of eight different courses on offer.
Decide which course would be the most suitable for the following teenagers.
For questions **6 – 10**, mark the correct letter (**A – H**).

6

Kevin has fun making things and he would like to learn to build models of ships and planes. He is also keen on learning about their history and he has free time for this at weekends.

G

7

Jemma is very interested in learning to draw and paint better. She mostly enjoys painting landscapes while listening to her favourite CDs and she wants a course that takes place on weekend mornings.

F

8

Eddie is artistic and creative and he wants go to classes on any evening except Monday to learn to play an instrument. He'd also like to be able to write song lyrics and put music to them.

H

9

Matt is very keen on wildlife, so he wants to learn about protecting nature where wild animals live. He can go to classes on Wednesday after school.

E

10

Janice can attend classes every Friday and Saturday afternoon and she wants to learn more about cooking and health. She loves making things and is also interested in knowing more about vegetables and fruit and how to grow them.

C

Courses for Teenagers

A **Art world** is a course which offers lessons on the history of art and can help you learn more about art in different periods of history. You don't need to be artistic to enjoy this course – all you need is to be interested in visiting museums and art galleries. We offer a two-hour class every weekend.

B **A taste of Europe** is a course which will allow the creative chef inside you to come out. Learn to cook French, Italian and Spanish cuisine and amaze your family and friends! During the course we learn the most important traditional dishes of these countries. Lessons are every Tuesday, Thursday and Friday evening.

C **Home-grown** is a modern cookery course that aims to teach youngsters how to prepare healthy and tasty food for themselves. Our recipes are easy to follow, the ingredients are always fresh and nutritious, and we also try to teach our students how to produce their own fruit and vegetables in their gardens. Our lessons are every Saturday afternoon.

D **Change the world** is an organisation which offers courses to children and teenagers who want to make a difference in the world. We show you how the environment is changing because of pollution and what is happening to the ice at the poles. We also discuss ways in which the younger generation can help change this situation. Our lessons are every Monday, Wednesday and Saturday evening.

E **Growing world** offers an amazing opportunity for young people to learn more about their planet and the animals that live on it. Learn all about the exciting and mysterious life forms that exist in our forests, deserts, mountains and valleys and how you can play a part in saving them and their habitats! Our course takes place every Monday or Wednesday, afternoon or evening.

F **Teen art** offers courses to teenagers and young adults who are interested not only in learning to paint and draw, but also in enjoying themselves while doing so. That's why, when we arrange where to draw and paint around the most beautiful parts of the city, we also choose some suitable music to take with us. If you want to spend your Saturday and Sunday mornings in a pleasant creative way, this is the right choice for you!

G **Small world** Learn all the secrets about how to make your own small-scale boats, aircraft and other vessels of World War II as well as finding out the fascinating stories behind them. Our course is on every Saturday morning.

H **On the rocks** is a course for young people which aims to teach the basics of rock music, rhythm, song writing and of course using the drums and the bass guitar correctly for a more dramatic effect! We offer lessons and practice every Friday and Saturday evening.

GUIDANCE FOR CANDIDATES

In Part 2, there are five short descriptions of different people. Then there are eight paragraphs (A–H). All the paragraphs are related to the same topic. You have to match the descriptions of the people to the paragraphs. For example, you may have to decide which type of holiday, product or activity would be best for each person. Each correct answer gets one mark. This part tests how well you can understand specific information and details.

Quickly read the five descriptions of people. This will give you a general idea of each person.

Now read the eight paragraphs (A–H). As you read, underline any key words or phrases so that you know what to look back for in the people descriptions. Underline any information you find in a text that matches a person. Look for words or phrases that say the same thing as one of the descriptions but in different words.

Sometimes you may find an answer straight away. Pencil in the answer but make sure that you check the answer again when you have completed the other questions. The correct paragraph (A–H) will match all parts of a particular description.

Remember to answer all the questions as you won't lose marks for a wrong answer.

READING PART 3

Questions 11 – 20

Look at the sentences below about skateboarding fashion.
Read the text on the opposite page to decide if each sentence is correct or incorrect.
If it is correct, mark **A**.
If it is not correct, mark **B**.

11	The people who started skateboarding did a different sport when the weather conditions were suitable.	(A)	B
12	Many young people like the skateboarding style.	(A)	B
13	'Baggy' means that the trousers are too uncomfortable to walk in.	A	(B)
14	Few adults understand how teenagers manage to skate in their clothes.	(A)	B
15	In the writer's opinion, skate clothing is ideal for doing sport.	(A)	B
16	Everybody who wants to wear baggy clothes should start skateboarding.	A	(B)
17	All the companies that sell clothes for skaters are from Australia.	A	(B)
18	A skater must pay more than fifty euros for a pair of skateboarding shoes.	A	(B)
19	There are places where you can find cheap clothes if you want to dress like a skater.	(A)	B
20	It is important for all skaters to look the same.	A	(B)

GUIDANCE FOR CANDIDATES

In Part 3, there are ten questions before one long text. Each question is a one-sentence statement about the text, and you have to decide if each statement is correct or incorrect according to what you read in the text. Remember that the questions are presented in the same order as the information appears in the text. Each correct answer gets one mark. This part tests how well you can find specific information and detail in one long factual text and whether you are able to understand which information is *not* needed in order to answer the questions.

Read the statements (11–20). Underline key words and phrases so that you know what you need to look for in the text.

Quickly read the text. This will help you get a general idea of what it's about.

As you work, you may find that you have already identified some of the answers. Pencil these in straight away, but remember to go back and check these answers as you read the text again.

Quickly read the text again to find each answer.

Underline the part of the text where you find the answers to questions. This will help you to check your answers at the end.

Don't worry about any unknown words; you won't need to understand every word to be able to choose the right answer. Just concentrate on whether a statement is true or not.

Don't spend a long time worrying about a question which you can't answer. Go on to the next question. If you have time, go back to the questions you couldn't answer when you have finished all the others.

Remember to give an answer for every question, even if you aren't sure. You will not lose marks for an incorrect answer.

Skateboarding is in fashion

Skateboarding is cool and popular for both boys and girls. Did you know that it first appeared in the 1950s and 1960s as a way for surfers to keep doing their favourite sport on land when there weren't any big waves? Since then, it has become popular all over the world, and so have the clothes that skaters wear.

Have a look around you the next time you go out and you'll notice that there are plenty of teenagers in your neighbourhood with the same urban skate look. They like dressing in big T-shirts, colourful trainers, baseball caps and baggy trousers, which are called baggy because they're very loose. In fact, they're usually so loose that they look two or three sizes bigger than what the person should be wearing.

Older people often laugh when they see a young skater passing by in baggy jeans because they think clothes like that can't be comfortable enough to walk or skateboard in. But they're wrong. One of the reasons skateboarding clothes are so fashionable is that it's so easy to move in them. They're really flexible, as well as being casual and stylish. That's why they're popular, not only with skaters, but also with those who like basketball and with young people in general. In other words, you don't have to be a skater to dress like one.

Most of the trendiest brands of skateboarding clothes and accessories are Australian. They're not exactly cheap, though. A pair of the most basic skateboarding shoes might cost you as much as €50! And to buy a plain T-shirt you'll need more than €60, or about €10 less if it's on special offer.

But don't worry! If you can't afford it, think about looking in a second-hand clothes shop for trousers, trainers, hats and so on. Don't be afraid to try something out that's a little different from what everyone else is wearing. As skaters say, 'Don't be a copycat; find your own style'.

READING PART 4

Questions 21 – 25

Read the text and questions below.
For each question, mark the correct letter **A**, **B**, **C** or **D**.

EATING AND HEALTH

Fifteen-year-old Peter Jones tells us about his eating habits and how they affected his health.

I've always been a very unhealthy eater, I'm sorry to say. When I was at primary school, I refused to eat my vegetables. My mother says it was impossible to make me eat anything I didn't like, so she gave me whatever I wanted, like chocolate and cake. My favourite was jam sandwiches. I think this is where my problems began.

When I first started secondary school three years ago, I didn't like the kind of food that was served as main meals. Instead, I chose what seemed like tastier snacks, which were not the healthiest options. Eating burgers and chips regularly, it wasn't a surprise when I put on a lot more weight.

I had to study really hard because I wanted to get good marks, so I stayed in with my books after school every day and never got any exercise. I did extra lessons at weekends and I didn't have time to think about what I was eating. When my parents were out working, they always left something healthy for my sister and me to eat, but I just made jam sandwiches and drank lemonade. I continued to get fatter.

The person who has helped me most is my big sister, Alice. She told me very clearly that I had to change or I would have serious health problems soon. She showed me a website with information about the damage that can be caused by eating the wrong foods. I didn't like it, but she encouraged me to go on a strict diet, with three meals a day and no snacks in between. I realised she was right. Sometimes you only understand something when somebody else explains it to you.

Now I've lost a lot of weight and I feel great, and everybody says I look healthier, too. I eat salads and fruit and I take regular exercise. My marks are still good, and I don't miss burgers or sweets. But sometimes, when Alice isn't looking, I have a jam sandwich. I still love them!

⌐GUIDANCE **FOR CANDIDATES**⌐

In Part 4, there is one long text followed by five multiple-choice questions with four options each. Each correct answer gets one mark. Part 4 tests how well you can understand why the text has been written, what the writer's opinion is, as well as detailed and overall meaning.

First read the text quickly to find out what the topic is and to get an idea of the general meaning. As you do this, you should think about *why* the writer wrote this text.

Now read the text again more carefully.

Now you are ready to answer the questions in order, checking that your answers agree with the text.

The first question is about the writer's purpose and the last one is about the overall meaning of the text. You may want to think about these two questions together.

Questions 2, 3 and 4 follow the order of the information in the text and one of them will be about an attitude or opinion.

Remember to answer all the questions as you won't lose marks for a wrong answer.

21 What is Peter doing in the text?

 A describing what he likes eating

 B talking about healthy food

 C explaining why you should eat proper meals

 D saying how his eating habits have changed

22 What do you learn about Peter from the text?

 A His favourite food has changed.

 B He likes all kinds of food.

 C He has learnt from his past.

 D His mother made him eat sweets.

23 What does he say about school?

 A His marks got worse because of his eating habits.

 B He didn't like doing sports at school.

 C He was so busy he didn't pay attention to his diet.

 D School food made him fatter.

24 What does Peter say about Alice?

 A She never eats unhealthy food.

 B She taught him something.

 C She understood that he was ill.

 D She took his advice about eating.

25 What might Peter say?

 A Although you might not like it, you should listen to other people's advice.

 B I feel better because I eat healthy food, but I wish I could eat fast food.

 C Eat whatever you like, but make sure you get some exercise.

 D Food can cause lots of problems, but it can make you happy, too.

READING PART 5

Questions 26 – 35

Read the text below and choose the correct word for each space.
For each question, mark the correct letter **A**, **B**, **C** or **D**.

Example:

0	**A** from	**B** between	**C** within	**D** around

Answer:

0	A	B	C	D
	☐	■	☐	☐

Life in Medieval England

Medieval times, or the Middle Ages, is the name given to the period in history **(0)** _____ the seventh and fifteenth centuries. Life in England then was very different **(26)** _____ the way we live now, especially for children. During this time, children were **(27)** _____ adults by the age of twelve.

When they **(28)** _____ this age, they began work and sometimes moved in with their employers. However, they had some **(29)** _____ time for leisure activities. The very young adults of the Middle Ages were quite social. **(30)** _____ a long day of working, they would **(31)** _____ time with their colleagues, family or friends, just like we do today. They also played board games, such as chess and backgammon, and they took **(32)** _____ in team sports similar to today's rugby and football.

A few activities, such **(33)** _____ hunting and horse-riding, were reserved for upper-class youths, mainly **(34)** _____ of the cost. Sword fighting was often not allowed in case the battles became dangerous. Practice with bows and arrows was **(35)** _____, though, as the skill was useful in times of war.

26	A in	B of	**C from**	D with
27	A believed	**B considered**	C thought	D supposed
28	A appeared	B came	C arrived	**D reached**
29	**A free**	B open	C long	D last
30	A When	B Since	**C After**	D Until
31	A play	B waste	C use	**D spend**
32	**A part**	B place	C time	D advantage
33	A like	**B as**	C that	D for
34	**A because**	B so	C regarding	D due
35	A supplied	B promised	**C encouraged**	D offered

GUIDANCE FOR CANDIDATES

In Part 5, you will read a short text with ten gaps and an example. For each gap, there is a multiple-choice question with four options. Each correct answer gets one mark. This part tests your knowledge of vocabulary and grammar such as prepositions, connectives, pronouns and modal verbs. For each gap, you have to decide which of the four words or phrases is correct. Option choices may be words with similar meanings, such as *total, amount, number* and *lot* or similar functions like *Since, Although, Despite* and *However*.

Read the text through quickly to get a general idea of the topic and meaning.

Now work through the ten questions. Make sure you read the complete sentence before you decide on the word to complete the gap. It's also a good idea to check that the other three options (which you have **not** chosen) do not and cannot fit in the gap. At the end, read the whole text again with your answers to check that it makes sense.

You should know all the words in the question options, but it's not enough to know the meanings of words – you also have to know how they are used. So learn words in phrases and remember what grammar and which other words go with them.

Remember to give an answer for every question, even if you aren't sure. You will not lose marks for an incorrect answer.

WRITING PART 1

Questions 1 – 5

Here are some sentences about a girl who goes to school.
For each question, complete the second sentence so that it means the same as the first.
Use no more than three words.
Write only the missing words.
You may use this page for any rough work.

Example:

0   Every day, Kelly goes to school by bus.
     Kelly _____ the bus to school every day.

Answer: | **0** | *takes* |

---

1   Kelly's history class is taught by Mr Hooper.

     Mr Hooper _____ *teaches* _____ Kelly's history class.

2   If Kelly does her homework, she won't get into trouble.

     Kelly will get into trouble _____ *unless* _____ she does her homework.

3   When Kelly started school, she bought a new school bag.

     Kelly has had a new school bag _____ *since* _____ she started school.

4   Kelly likes art more than science.

     Kelly _____ *prefers* _____ art to science.

5   All the teachers at Kelly's school are good.

     There _____ *aren't any / are not any / are no* _____ bad teachers at Kelly's school.

GUIDANCE FOR CANDIDATES

There are three parts to the Writing test with a total of 25 marks. Parts 1 and 2 have five marks each and Part 3 is worth fifteen marks. Remember that the Writing section of Paper 1 is just as important as the Reading section: each section is worth 25% of the total exam.

It's important that you give yourself time (about 40 minutes) to complete all three parts of the Writing section. In Parts 2 and 3, you should think about who you're writing to and why, and write in an appropriate style.

You can write with joined-up letters or not; in UPPER CASE or lower case. You cannot use a dictionary in the exam. Always give yourself time to re-read what you have written to check and make any changes.

In Part 1, there are five sentences which are all related to the same topic. For each question, you have a complete sentence and a gapped sentence underneath it. You should write between one and three words to complete the gap so that the finished sentence means the same as the sentence above it. Sometimes there may be more than one correct answer. Each correct answer gets one mark. This part tests how well you can use different grammar structures.

The instructions for this part tell you the topic of the sentences. Take note of this as it will help you to understand the sentences better. There is an example to show you what to do. Do not write the example answer on the answer sheet.

Short forms such as *don't* (*do not*) count as two words, but *can't* (*cannot*) counts as one word. If you write more than three words, your answer is marked as wrong. Be very careful with your spelling in this part of the test as you will lose marks if you spell the words wrongly.

First read the example so you know what you have to do.

Now begin the exercise. Read the first sentence carefully. Ask yourself, *What are they testing here?* For example, in question 1 here the first sentence is in the passive (*Kelly's history class is taught by Mr Hooper*) but the second sentence is not. This means that you have to rewrite the sentence using the active voice. You need to focus on what you know about the passive in order to answer the question correctly.

Underline the words in the first sentence that have to be changed to complete the second sentence.

Complete the second sentence.

Read the first sentence and the completed second sentence again. Do the two sentences mean exactly the same thing?

Check that you have not used more than three words to complete the gap.

WRITING PART 2

Question 6

It was your birthday last week and your favourite uncle sent you some money to buy a present that you wanted.

Write a 'thank you' note to your uncle. In your note, you should:

- tell your uncle what you bought with the money
- say why you like it
- say how you are going to use it.

Write **35–45 words**.

Students' own answers

⌐GUIDANCE FOR CANDIDATES⌐

In Part 2, there is one question that you have to answer. It consists of an instruction or maybe a short text that you have to respond to. The instructions will tell you who you are writing to and why. You must write an email, a note, or a postcard. There are three specific items which you must include in your writing. These are clearly listed so you won't forget what they are. You should write between 35 and 45 words.

There are five marks for this part. You can score the full five marks even if you make some mistakes, as long as the meaning is clear and you have included all the three points.

You should practise writing notes, short texts and emails that are of the right length in class. You will lose marks if your answer is too short or too long. You need about fifteen minutes for this part of the test so you should have time to make some notes before you start.

Read the instructions carefully, and the text if there is one.

Underline the key words in the instructions and text. Ask yourself these questions: *Who are you writing to? Why are you writing?*

Read the three points carefully and make short notes of your ideas next to each one. Make a note of any useful words or phrases that you want to include.

Complete your writing. Don't forget that you must write your answer on the special answer sheet.

When you have finished, read through what you have written and check that you have included all three of the points you were given.

Finally, check for any grammar or spelling mistakes.

WRITING PART 3

Write an answer to **one** of the questions (**7** or **8**) in this part.
Write your answer in about **100 words**.

Question 7

- This is part of a letter you received from an English friend.

> We're doing a school project about famous pop
> stars from different countries. Who's the most
> popular pop singer in your country? What can
> you tell me about him/her?

- Now write a **letter** to your friend.

Question 8

- Your English teacher has asked you to write a story.

- Your story must begin with this sentence:

    I turned on my computer and started writing the email as fast as I could.

- Write your **story**.

Students' own answers

⌈GUIDANCE **FOR CANDIDATES**⌋

In Part 3, you have a choice of writing either an informal letter or a story. The length should be around 100 words. If your writing is less than 80 words, you will lose marks.

For the letter option, you are given an extract of a letter from a friend, which provides the topic you will write about. A couple of questions may be included to help you focus your ideas. You will lose marks if you don't keep to the topic.

To do well in this task you should practise writing letters and emails to friends using appropriate opening and closing phrases and linking words. Think about how to organise a letter so it reads smoothly.

You might choose the story option if you have a good imagination. You are given a title or an opening sentence. It is up to you how you develop your story and what you include, but remember it has to be a story, not just a description of a place or a person, so something must happen.

Be careful that you write in the correct person; if the title of a story is about a girl called Lily, then don't write it in the first person about yourself.

If an opening sentence is given for a story, remember that you *must* write this as your *first* sentence.

In Part 3, you are tested on how well you can use vocabulary, expressions and different grammar structures to communicate. You won't lose marks for small spelling mistakes that don't make it difficult to understand your story or letter, so be ambitious and use some interesting language. Use both shorter and longer sentences, and try not to repeat the same vocabulary too often. Make sure your ideas are logically linked so that they are easy to follow and sound natural.

LISTENING PART 1

Questions 1 – 7

There are seven questions in this part.
For each question, choose the correct answer **A**, **B** or **C**.

Example: Where did the boy leave his camera?

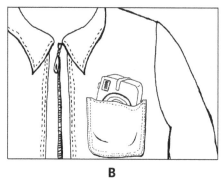
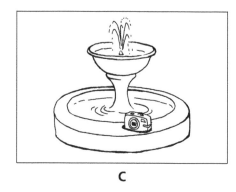

A   B   C

1 What has the boy already eaten today?

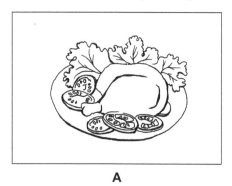
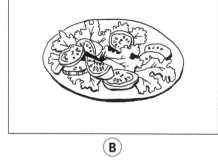
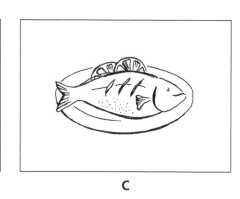

A   B   C

2 What does the man want to buy?

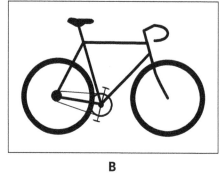

A   B   C

3 What does the students' first teacher look like now?

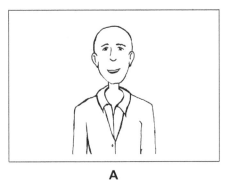

A

B

C

4 What is the weather like now?

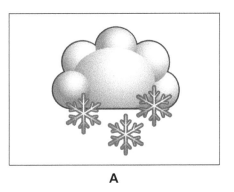

A

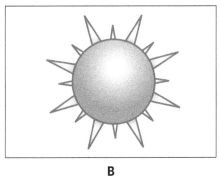

B

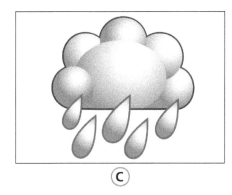

C

5 What is the programme about?

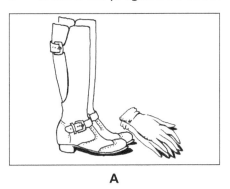

A

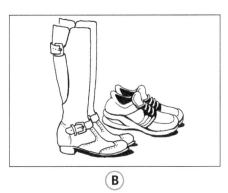

B

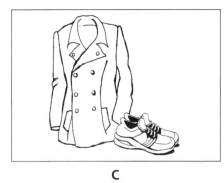

C

6 What do they need to buy?

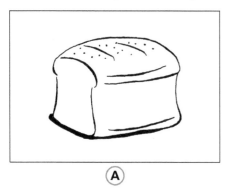

A

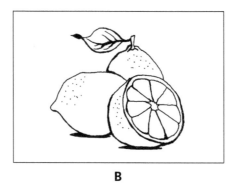

B

C

7 What sport are they talking about?

A

B

C

GUIDANCE FOR CANDIDATES

You probably listen to quite a lot of different things in English. You watch films, hear songs and see English language TV programmes. You've listened to your teacher and classmates speaking English and you have had listening practice with CDs in class. You are already well prepared for this part of the test.

There are four parts in the Listening Paper with 25 questions altogether, each worth one mark. You will hear the instructions written on your paper for each part on the CD and you will have time to look over the questions before each part begins. Use this time to read the questions or look at the picture options. This will help you to understand what kind of recording you are going to listen to and what kind of information you are listening for. It is important that you do plenty of listening practice in class so that you know what to expect in each part of the test and what you have to do.

Remember you will hear each part twice, so don't panic if you're not sure of any answer the first time you hear it. For Part 1, there is an example to show you what you have to do. You should write your answers on the question paper as you listen.

The test takes about 30 minutes and you'll have six minutes at the end to transfer your answers to the answer sheet.

In Part 1, you hear seven short monologues or dialogues on common daily subjects. For each short recording, there is a question followed by three picture options. You must listen and choose the picture option which answers the question. You will hear the recording for each question twice before it moves on to the next question.

The questions begin with words such as *Which, What, Who, Where* and *How*. Each correct answer gets one mark. This part tests your understanding of specific information within a monologue or dialogue.

There is an example at the beginning of Part 1 to remind you of what you have to do.

During the first listening, listen carefully, think about the general idea and use a pencil to circle the possible answer. During the second listening, check your answer. Don't get 'stuck' on a question. If you know you've just missed the answer to a question, don't spend time thinking about what it might have been. You need to move on to the next question.

If you're really not sure of an answer, make a guess – don't leave any answers blank. Remember that you don't lose marks for incorrect answers.

LISTENING PART 2

Questions 8 – 13

You will hear a teenager named Henry Clark talking about a talent show that he recently took part in. For each question, choose the correct answer **A**, **B** or **C**.

8   Why didn't Henry like the idea of a talent show?

   A He was afraid of audiences.

   B He wasn't comfortable with his voice.

   C He had never been in a competition.

9   Why did Henry decide to do the talent show?

   A He thought it would be good practice.

   B His mother made him enter the show.

   C He realised the show would be fun.

10   Why did Henry stop having lessons with Ms Vine?

   A He didn't think she was a good teacher.

   B He and his family moved to another town.

   C She wasn't available to give lessons any more.

11   When Henry had a sore throat, he

   A decided to leave the competition.

   B just kept practising.

   C realised he couldn't give up.

12   What did Henry do the day before the show?

   A relaxed and took it easy

   B practised to make up lost hours

   C wrote down the words to his song

13   How did Henry feel when he was singing?

   A worried

   B calm

   C tired

GUIDANCE FOR CANDIDATES

In Part 2, you will hear either a monologue or a dialogue where there is one main speaker, for example, an interview on the radio. There are six multiple-choice questions and for each question you choose the correct answer A, B or C. You will hear the recording twice. Each correct answer gets one mark. You need to understand specific information from the recording, but sometimes you may also need to identify somebody's opinion or attitude.

Always use the time given to read through the questions. This will help you to focus on what you need to listen for. The more you can predict about what you're going to hear, the more you'll understand when you actually listen to the recording.

During the first listening, make a light pencil mark on any answers which you think are correct. When you hear the recording again, check your answers and add any that you missed the first time.

As you listen, don't focus on any words or phrases in the recording that you don't understand. Don't let these words stop you from listening to the rest of the recording. If you get 'stuck' on one word or short part of the recording, you will not listen to the rest of the recording.

If you hear a word or phrase that is in one of the answer options, this doesn't mean this option is the correct one. Listen for the whole meaning.

During the second listening, you can concentrate more closely on finding the best option for each question and check your answers from the first listening.

Remember – never leave a question unanswered. If you don't know the answer, then guess. You will not lose marks for a wrong answer, but you might be lucky and guess the correct answer.

LISTENING PART 3

Questions 14 – 19

You will hear some information about a race.
For each question, fill in the missing information in the numbered space.

School fun run

Date: 26th April

Starting time: **(14)** _____ *half past ten / 10.30* _____

First fun run happened: **(15)** _____ *thirty/30 years* _____ ago

This year's money is for: e-readers for digital **(16)** _____ *library* _____

To take part in the race you need: **(17)** _____ *(a pair of) trainers* _____ and a tracksuit

Races

Full race: 6 km

Other races on that day: a **(18)** _____ *4/four* _____ km race and a 2 km race

Special races for younger children

Prizes

First prize: a **(19)** _____ *(brand new) bicycle/bike* _____

Second and third prizes: roller skates

Souvenir T-shirt for all the students who take part

⌐GUIDANCE FOR CANDIDATES⌐

In Part 3, you will hear a monologue, that is, somebody speaking alone. You have a page of notes with six gaps which you must complete. You should complete the gaps with single words, numbers or very short phrases to complete the missing information. You will hear the recording twice. Each correct answer gets one mark. In this part you need to find information and understand it.

The answers you need are exactly the words you hear on the recording, so you're listening for specific information. You don't need to change the words or write them in a different way. Remember, the answers will be short phrases, a word or number. Don't write long answers.

In the pause before you listen, look through the questions to predict the sort of language and information you are going to hear. This will help you to focus on the missing information that you are listening for.

For example, in question 14 in this test you are obviously listening for a time (the time that the fun run starts).

As you listen for the first time, pencil in any answers you hear. Try to focus on the information you need and try not to worry about other things you hear which are not necessary in order to complete the gaps.

During the second listening, check your answers and complete any answers which you didn't get the first time.

LISTENING PART 4

Questions 20 – 25

Look at the six sentences for this part.
You will hear a conversation between a girl, Carla, and a boy, Jason, where they give their opinions on wearing school uniforms.
Decide if each sentence is correct or incorrect.
If it is correct, choose the letter **A** for **YES**. If it is not correct, choose the letter **B** for **NO**.

		YES	NO
20	Carla last met Jason several months ago.	(A)	B
21	Jason says that Carla's uniform looks awful.	A	(B)
22	Carla believes that wearing a school uniform makes life easier.	(A)	B
23	Jason wants to look different to other people.	(A)	B
24	Carla thinks uniforms are a bad idea because everybody looks the same.	A	(B)
25	Jason's opinion about uniforms changes in the end.	(A)	B

GUIDANCE FOR CANDIDATES

In Part 4, you will hear a conversation between two people about an everyday topic. The two speakers are usually a man and a woman. You are given six statements and you must decide whether the statements are true or false depending on what you hear. You should circle A for 'Yes' (true) or B for 'No' (false). You will hear the recording twice. Each correct answer gets one mark. You have to listen for detailed meaning and be able to understand the opinions of the speakers in order to be able to select the correct option.

During the pause before you hear the recording, it is a good idea to underline the key words in the six statements. This will help you to focus on what you are going to listen to and the ideas you need to identify.

For example, in question 1 here, you might underline *last met* and *more than a year ago*. Because of this you know you need to pay attention to when the two people met for the last time.

As you listen for the first time, try to understand the general meaning and circle A or B. When you listen again, check your answers carefully. You may need to change one or two of them if there was something you didn't understand correctly before.

Don't forget that when you have finished all four parts of the Listening test you will need to copy your answers onto the separate answer sheet. You will have six minutes to do this.

SPEAKING PART 1

2–3 minutes (3–4 minutes for a group of three)

Phase 1

Interlocutor *(Say to both candidates)*	Good morning/afternoon/evening. Can I have your mark sheets, please? I'm _____ and this is _____. He/She is just going to listen to us.
(Say to Candidate A)	Now, what's your name? Thank you.
(Say to Candidate B)	And what's your name? Thank you.

Students' own answers

Back-up prompts

Interlocutor *(Say to Candidate B)*	Candidate B, what's your surname? How do you spell it? Thank you.	How do you write your family / second name?
(Say to Candidate A)	And, Candidate A, what's your surname? How do you spell it? Thank you.	How do you write your family / second name?

Interlocutor *(Ask the following questions. Ask Candidate A first.)*	Where do you live / come from? Do you study English at school? Do you like it? Thank you.	Do you live in *(name of local area)*? Do you have English lessons?
(Repeat for Candidate B.)		

Phase 2
Interlocutor *(Select one or more questions from the list to ask each candidate. Use candidates' names throughout. Ask Candidate B first.)*

How many brothers or sisters have you got?
What do your parents do?
Tell us about your favourite person in your family.
What do you enjoy doing with your family?
Thank you.

Introduction to Part 2
In the next part, you are going to talk to each other.

GUIDANCE FOR CANDIDATES

In the speaking test, you will be with another candidate and there will be two examiners, but only one of them will speak to you. There are four parts to the test which lasts about twelve minutes. Occasionally, there may be three candidates. In this case, the test is the same but takes a little longer.

The examiner is there to ask you questions and help you to do the best you can. Your job is to know what you have to do in each part and speak as naturally as you can. You won't pass if you only answer in one word or are mostly silent. If you get stuck or can't remember a word, don't panic; try and use other words to explain what you want to say. Don't worry about making mistakes; just think about getting your message across and responding to the examiner and your partner appropriately. You can ask the examiner or your partner to repeat any instruction, question or answer that you don't understand at any time during the test.

Arrive at the examination centre in plenty of time. When you go into the room, make sure there's no chewing gum in your mouth!

Remember: Be polite, don't give one word answers and, at the end of the test, don't ask if you passed. The examiner won't tell you!

In Part 1 of the test, the examiner asks you your name and asks you to spell your surname. The examiner will then ask you some general questions about yourself.

A good answer to the question *Where do you live?* might be *I live in a small village called Stoupa which is near Kalamata.* That's all you need to say. You shouldn't say something you've learnt which is not relevant to the question, such as *I live in a house which has two floors and consists of a living room, kitchen and three bedrooms.*

You should feel confident in this part of the test because you don't need to think up answers. You know what the questions are going to be and you can practise interviews in class.

SPEAKING PART 2

2–3 minutes (3 minutes for a group of three)

Best way to make friends in a new place

Interlocutor
(Say to both candidates)

See pictures on page 169

I'm going to describe a situation to you.
A friend of yours recently went to live in another town and he doesn't know anyone there. Talk together about the best ways he can make friends in his new town.
Here is a picture with some ideas to help you.

I'll say that again.
A friend of yours recently went to live in another town and he doesn't know anyone there. Talk together about the best ways he can make friends in his new town.
All right? Talk together.

(Allow the candidates enough time to complete the task without intervention. Prompt only if necessary.)

Thank you.

Students' own answers

GUIDANCE FOR CANDIDATES

In Part 2, you're given a situation and are shown some pictures, such as photos or drawings, which you have to talk about with your partner. While you are looking at the pictures, the examiner will repeat the instructions, so if you didn't understand what he/she said you will be able to check again when the instructions are repeated.

Remember that this is not a monologue; it's a conversation between you and your partner. You have to listen to what your partner says and respond. You discuss, share opinions, agree and disagree, suggest and recommend.

Remember that you're not supposed to describe the pictures in detail; you're using them as ideas to discuss the issue and come to a conclusion.

Don't spend time looking silently at the prompts trying to decide which one is the best option. Start your discussion immediately and talk about why some options are not so good as well as why some are better. For example, *OK. I think this option is a good idea. What do you think?*

It doesn't matter whether you agree with each other. What's important is that you use the pictures to have a discussion with your partner to try to reach a decision.

You need to use language for agreeing and disagreeing and questioning in this part. It's fine to disagree with your partner, but be polite! Say, *I'm sorry, but I don't agree with what you said, because* … and then give a reason why.

Try to move the discussion forward. Do lots of practice in class where you have to come to an agreement using phrases such as *Yes, I suppose you're right, but … . Why don't we …?* and *How about this option?*

SPEAKING PART 3

3 minutes (4 minutes for a group of three)

Interlocutor *(Say to both candidates)*	Now, I'd like each of you to talk on your own about something. I'm going to give each of you a photograph of teenagers **playing sport**.
See photo A on page 170	*(Candidate A)*, here is your photograph. Please show it to *(Candidate B)*, but I'd like you to talk about it. *(Candidate B)*, you just listen. I'll give you your photograph in a moment. *(Candidate A)*, please tell us what you can see in your photograph.
Candidate A	*(Approximately 1 minute)*

(If there is a need to intervene, prompts rather than direct questions should be used.)

Interlocutor See photo B on page 170	Thank you. Now, *(Candidate B)*, here is your photograph. It also shows teenagers playing sport. Please show it to *(Candidate A)* and tell us what you can see in the photograph.
Candidate B	*(Approximately 1 minute)*

(If there is a need to intervene, prompts rather than direct questions should be used.)

Interlocutor	Thank you.

Students' own answers

⌐GUIDANCE FOR CANDIDATES⌐

In Part 3, you speak on your own for about a minute. You'll be given a colour photograph and all you have to do is to describe it. Then your partner will do the same with a different photo which is related to the same topic.

Imagine you're describing the photo to someone who can't see it – say as much as you can about the people or places shown and try to use more than very simple vocabulary and structures. Talk about the people, the colours, the weather, and whatever is happening in the photo. Don't just say something like, *I can see some boys. There is a football.* Say something more like this: *Well, I can see some boys who are playing football. There are two teams. One team is wearing yellow T-shirts and blue shorts and the other team is wearing green T-shirts and shorts.*

When you give an answer, think about *who, what, where, when, how and why.* If you answer some of these questions in your response, it will be much fuller than if you only answer with a short sentence such as, *They are playing football.*

If you get stuck on a word, it doesn't matter as long as you keep going. For example, it's fine to say: *Oh, I'm afraid I don't know what that thing in the corner is called, but it's something you use in the garden.*

In class, do lots of practice in pairs or groups describing photos you bring in from magazines or print from the Internet.

SPEAKING PART 4

3 minutes (3–4 minutes for a group of three)

Interlocutor
(Say to both candidates)

Your photographs showed teenagers **playing sport**. Now, I'd like you to talk together about a sport **you** have played in the **past** and another sport you would like to play in the **future**.

(Allow the candidates enough time to complete the task without intervention. Prompt only if necessary.)

Thank you. That's the end of the test.

Students' own answers

⌐GUIDANCE **FOR CANDIDATES**⌐

In Part 4, you are going to have a discussion with your partner on the topic you discussed in Part 3. You will talk together about your likes/dislikes, opinions or experiences.

The examiner won't usually take part in the discussion during this part, but may ask extra questions to help you and your partner to keep talking.

Don't forget that this is not a monologue. As well as talking about yourself, you should ask what your partner thinks and show interest in what he or she says.

When you talk about the topic, you should be able to give reasons for your opinions.

Practice Test 2

READING PART 1

Questions 1 – 5

Look at the text in each question.
What does it say?
Mark the correct letter **A**, **B** or **C**.

Example:

0

> **FOR RENT**
> Nice two-bedroom flat in Chelsea area
> Close to bus station, all new kitchen and bathroom
> Central heating, parking space available
> Call Jenny on 569-9993 for more information

The advert says the flat

A   is cheap.

B   is near public transport.

C   is suitable for two people.

Answer:

1

> **DIVING CENTRE**
>
> Training begins at six o'clock.
>
> Please visit the front desk 30 minutes before training starts to pick up the diving equipment.

A   Training begins at six and lasts for 30 minutes.

B   Divers must visit the front desk to fill out some forms.

C   Some things need to be collected at the front desk first.

2

> **Macaroni Cheese**
> Boil 3 litres of water in pan.
> Add macaroni and boil for 10 – 12 minutes, stirring occasionally.
> When macaroni is ready, place it in strainer.
> Heat butter in pan, stir in flour, then add milk and cheese.
> Mix well, then add macaroni.

A   The macaroni should be stirred more than once while it cooks.

B   The cheese, butter and milk go into the water.

C   Just before the water boils, add the macaroni.

3

> 5.20 PM
>
> Erica,
> I'm not feeling well and can't come to dance practice. Can you remember to get me an entry form for the competition? Will take an aspirin and go to bed now. See you tomorrow at school if I'm feeling better.
> Janet

What should Erica do?

A   put Janet's name down for a competition

B   get a document for Janet

C   bring Janet an aspirin

4

To: Greg
From: Mark

Hi Greg,

Just wanted to say I bought the tickets for our trip. I also printed the boarding passes for our flight. If you like, I can keep yours with me, or give them to you tomorrow.

Mark

A Mark is going to keep Greg's ticket and boarding pass for him.

B Mark wants to know if Greg wants Mark to buy plane tickets.

C Mark is offering to hold on to Greg's ticket and boarding pass.

5

Hi Dad,

Mum called and said she's picking up your suit from the dry cleaner's today, so there's no need for you to do it. She also wanted me to remind you that you have a doctor's appointment tomorrow at 10 am.

Kim

What should Kim's dad do?

A contact her mum about a doctor's appointment

B meet her mum at the dry cleaner's to get his suit

C remember to go somewhere next morning

TIPS

In Part 1, you have five very short texts to read and you have to choose the option **A**, **B** or **C** that gives the main message. Make sure you read the example first and that you understand why **B** is the right answer (*near public transport* means the same as *close to bus station*). The correct answer always says something that is important in the text in a different way.

Remember to quickly read the text before you look at the options, then make sure you read all three options. Sometimes you can easily decide that one option is wrong. In the example, **A** can't be right because the text says nothing about rent or costs.

Don't choose an option just because it has a word which is in the text. Option **C** in the example says the flat is suitable for two people and the text says there are two bedrooms. For example, a couple or two students can share a bedroom, so the flat may be suitable for more than two people.

Don't worry if you don't know a word in the text. For question 2, you don't need to know what a *strainer* is to get the right answer.

Be careful that you don't choose an option that is not given in the text. In question 3, you may think it's a good idea that Erica should take medicine to her friend who is ill, but does the text say this is what Erica should do?

Read any questions above the text carefully. For example, question 5 asks what Kim's dad will do, not what Kim will do. It's easy to misread a question in the exam so take care.

READING PART 2

Questions 6 – 10

The teenagers below are choosing summer camps.
On the opposite page, there are descriptions of eight summer camps for young people.
Decide which summer camp would be the most suitable for the following teenagers.
For questions **6 – 10**, mark the correct letter (**A – H**).

6

Stefan would like to go to a summer camp that offers outdoor activities. He also enjoys water sports and would like to go somewhere with swimming facilities.

B

7

Harriet is interested in nature and would like to go to a summer camp that is located in the countryside. She is also an animal lover and enjoys bird watching.

D

8

Thomas loves sports and would like to go to a summer camp that offers different sporting activities. He is also keen on cycling so would like to go somewhere with good cycle routes.

E

9

Nina is interested in art and drama and would like to go to a camp where she can improve her skills. She also likes hiking so would like to go to a camp outside the city.

F

10

Craig would like to go to an adventure sports summer camp. He is interested in trying more challenging sports. He also loves camping and spending time outside.

H

Summer Camps

A Become the new Tom Cruise or Angelina Jolie at **Camp Act!** Full-day courses on acting, drama and film will help you make the most of your skills and talent. Theatre and Film trips are included in the price of the summer course, so what are you waiting for? Become a star this summer!

B **Camp Number 1** offers a range of sports and activities for everyone. Set in a huge park just north of the city, the camp benefits from a large lake, perfect for sailing, canoeing and swimming. We believe in the great outdoors; that's why we spend most of the time doing fun and challenging activities out in the open air!

C **Camp Central** is the only sports summer camp you'll ever need! With our huge gymnasium, sports hall and heated indoor swimming pool, you won't be bored. There are hundreds of sports to choose from and plenty of exercise classes for everyone. We also run some outdoor trips, depending on the weather.

D Set in beautiful woods, **Teen Camp** is the perfect place for anyone who loves to be outside. The area has long woodland paths for hiking or bike rides and is full of strange and wonderful forest creatures. Our night walks make sure that you don't miss the owls, bats and badgers that sleep in the day but come out at night.

E Leave football and tennis behind, and try something new at **Active Camp**. We offer sports like fishing and golf, as well as ice hockey in our indoor sports centre. Our best feature is that we're situated in the hilly countryside, which means that mountain biking is a must!

F **Talent Camp** is perfect for anyone who wants to improve their natural talents. Our experts run daily classes on how to write, act, sing and dance. We also know that talent needs inspiration. Our daily outdoor 'walk and draw' sessions over fields, through valleys and across rivers provide the very best of nature for the young and talented.

G **Sci-Camp** is the camp for you if you just love science, nature and the environment. The summer camp takes place at one of the top universities, where you can use all the latest science equipment and do your own experiments. Regular day trips into the country mean that you get a good look at the natural world too.

H **Extreme Camp** is for all of you who want to try more exciting things this summer. Our programme lets campers try extreme sports like paragliding, kite-surfing and bungee jumping. All activities take place outside. Campers should bring their own tents and be ready for anything!

READING PART 3

Questions 11 – 20

Look at the sentences below about online computer games.
Read the text on the opposite page to decide if each sentence is correct or incorrect.
If it is correct, mark **A**.
If it is not correct, mark **B**.

---

11   Online computer games appeal to young people for two main reasons.   (A)   B

12   These types of games are only available locally.   A   (B)

13   Most people play these kinds of games to meet others and make friends.   A   (B)

14   People who play these games know that they have at least one shared interest.   (A)   B

15   Playing these games means you can be a member of an online social group.   (A)   B

16   The variety of games on offer is quite limited.   A   (B)

17   Even without access to the Internet, people can enjoy these kinds of games.   A   (B)

18   People used to think that playing computer games was unsociable.   (A)   B

19   By playing these games, young people have opportunities that they don't get elsewhere.   (A)   B

20   This is the only example of the Internet being used by people who want to meet others.   A   (B)

TIPS

In Part 3, you should read the statements first, then look for the answers in the text. The information you need is in the same order in the text as it appears in the questions, which means you'll find the answer to question 11 before question 12 and so on.

Question 12: Here you're looking for a particular word or phrase in the text that agrees or disagrees with the statement. Be careful though – these games *are* available locally, but are they *only* available locally as the statement says? What is the phrase in the text that gives you the answer? The word *only* is also important in question 20.

Online Gaming

A new type of game has hit our computers in recent years, one which combines two of the most popular teenage interests: computer games and online chat. Online games allow players to get involved in the world of the game: complete missions, fight battles and score points, and at the same time chat to other players. What is special about this is that the characters in the games are controlled by real people; people who are playing the same games from their own bedrooms in countries all over the world!

This means that when you play these games, you are actually interacting with people just like you, and not the programmed systems of traditional computer games. Players interact with each other as much or as little as they want. Some teenagers limit their social 'chat' to game purposes, whether that's teaming up with another character to fight a common enemy or passing the football across the pitch in order to set up a goal for their team. Others, however, are now playing this sort of game for social reasons.

'It's fun talking to people from other countries,' says Luke, 16, from London. 'Knowing that you both love the game means that you already have something in common. Of course, you should stick to games that are suitable for your age group. I'm also very careful about who I chat to and I never give personal information to strangers.' Jenny, 18, from Scotland says, 'Some of my best friends are people that I've met in online games. We log on and talk about everything from school to hobbies, and if we don't feel like talking, well, we just play!' Thousands of teenagers all over the world are now enjoying this 'social gaming' as they join the online community of players.

Does it ever get boring? I doubt it! There is a huge range of interactive games available for all ages, including role playing games (RPGs) where you play as a character, board games like chess or backgammon, and even sports games. Of course, you need a good connection to the Web and a computer that supports games, but apart from that you're ready to go. You don't even need to count your pocket money because there are hundreds of free games online.

Online gaming is changing the way we think about computer games. They are no longer a reason for teenagers to be locked in their rooms and not socialising – quite the opposite! These kinds of games give young people the opportunity to engage with others, to socialise and to meet people that otherwise they might never have had the chance to meet. I suppose we shouldn't be too surprised as this is just another one of the many ways that the Internet is being used for social reasons. Despite its attractions, though, it should never replace getting out and spending time with your school friends.

READING PART 4

Questions 21 – 25

Read the text and questions below.
For each question, mark the correct letter **A**, **B**, **C** or **D**.

Living with Tourette's

Fifteen-year-old Michelle talks about a medical condition that affects about one child in every hundred.

When I tell people I've got Tourette's Syndrome, most people think that I'm going to start swearing at them or saying horrible things. That's how Tourette's is always shown in films and on TV, but actually only about ten per cent of Tourette's sufferers have no control over the bad language they use. Luckily, I'm not in that group.

Tourette's Syndrome is a condition that starts and develops in childhood. The main symptoms are tics. These are either small sharp facial or body movements, or sounds. The problem is that a Tourette's sufferer has no control over them and, while they might only be small movements like jerking your head, it can be pretty embarrassing, believe me! The worst thing is not knowing when this is going to happen, and if I go out with people that I don't really know, I get quite self-conscious.

No one really knows what causes Tourette's and, at the moment, there isn't a cure for it. It's not so bad though, because the tics don't stop me doing anything I want to do, and actually I don't even take medication for them. Lots of people who have Tourette's only have mild cases, and surprisingly, most sufferers are actually school children. They suffer from tics like coughing, sniffing, blinking their eyes a lot and strange facial movements. It usually gets worse when children are between ten and twelve years old in their last years of primary school, just when they are starting to worry about what other people think of them.

Luckily, only about fifty per cent of children who suffer with Tourette's continue to have it when they grow up. The tics usually stop by the time teenagers are eighteen, which means that many adults who had the condition as children are fine now. That's quite a comforting thought and, even though I'm used to my condition, I hope I'm one of the lucky ones who doesn't have to deal with it when I'm older.

TIPS

In Part 4, you'll read about someone's opinion about something. Don't worry if you don't know a word in the title. You've probably never heard of *Tourette's*, but the sub-heading tells you that it is a medical condition.

Read through the text quickly before you look at the multiple-choice questions to get the general idea of what the text is about and why it was written. The first question asks you about the reason the writer had for writing this piece. So, as you're reading, think about whether the writer is explaining, describing, advising or complaining.

When you read the five multiple-choice questions, remember you'll find the answers to questions 22, 23 and 24 in the order of the information in the text.

Question 25: The last question is about the general meaning of the whole text. All of the options may be true or partly true, but you have to decide which one <u>best</u> describes what Michelle says overall.

21 What is Michelle doing in the text?

A explaining what Tourette's is and how it affects people

B giving advice for Tourette's sufferers

C complaining about people who don't understand Tourette's

D describing how she had Tourette's as a child

22 What does Michelle say is most difficult to deal with?

A getting new people to understand her condition

B feeling uneasy about her condition when she is out

C the unexpected nature of the tics

D not being in control of her body

23 Why does Michelle think Tourette's is particularly difficult for school children?

A They all have to take medicine.

B It gets worse when they are at an age when they feel self-conscious.

C It stops them doing things they enjoy.

D There is no cure for Tourette's Syndrome.

24 What is Michelle's attitude towards Tourette's and her future?

A She doesn't mind having it because she is used to it.

B If she has children, she hopes they won't have Tourette's.

C She hopes that it won't affect her later on in life.

D She is confident that she will be able to manage the condition.

25 Which of these best describes what Michelle says?

A Tourette's symptoms are easy to cure in adults, but young people are more affected by the tics.

B Tourette's is an embarrassing and difficult condition to deal with, especially for teenagers and adults.

C Tourette's isn't as serious as they say on TV, but many young people have to face it.

D Tourette's is a misunderstood condition that is worse in teenagers, but which doesn't always continue into adulthood.

Practice Test 2

READING PART 5

Questions 26 – 35

Read the text below and choose the correct word for each space.
For each question, mark the correct letter **A**, **B**, **C** or **D**.

Example:

0 A Since **B** After **C** Until **D** Before

Answer:

0	A	B	C	D
	■	☐	☐	☐

Animated cartoons

One of the first cartoons ever to be made was *Felix the Cat* in 1919. The black and white cartoon had no sound, but the basic animation was immediately a hit. **(0)** _____ then, cartoons have become more and more popular, **(26)** _____ with the introduction of Mickey Mouse in 1928.

Cartoons used to be **(27)** _____ in the cinemas before the main film started, but once television was **(28)** _____, cartoons became popular at home, and with people of **(29)** _____ ages. It didn't take long for the cartoon industry to take off, and soon animation companies all over America were making short cartoons **(30)** _____ TV.

The next big step for animation came in 1937 when Disney made the first long cartoon film, *Snow White and the Seven Dwarfs*. **(31)** _____ that the film was a huge success, Disney released dozens more animated films for young children and families.

These days computers and technology are used to **(32)** _____ cartoons and animated films, and the results are amazing! Films like *How to Train Your Dragon*, *Happy Feet 2* and *Toy Story 3* are just **(33)** _____ of the films **(34)** _____ use this new technology.

Cartoons and animated films have grown in success over the years and now big cinemas all over the **(35)** _____ regularly show animated films.

26	**A** definitely	**B** especially	**C** mainly	**D** mostly
27	**A** presented	**B** filmed	**C** run	**D** shown
28	**A** started	**B** discovered	**C** made	**D** invented
29	**A** all	**B** every	**C** each	**D** both
30	**A** in	**B** for	**C** with	**D** on
31	**A** Wondering	**B** Looking	**C** Seeing	**D** Watching
32	**A** make	**B** fix	**C** construct	**D** build
33	**A** few	**B** some	**C** little	**D** part
34	**A** who	**B** where	**C** which	**D** what
35	**A** region	**B** world	**C** planet	**D** earth

TIPS

Remember to read the text before you look at the options and, as you read, think of what word *might* fit each gap. Remember to read the whole sentence before deciding on your word. Then look at the multiple-choice options and read the text again.

Always look at the example. If you don't read the whole sentence, you might think more than one word is correct because they can go before the word *then*. However, only *Since* is correct because the rest of the sentence continues in the present perfect.

Question 34: When you read through the text without looking at the options, you might think that the correct answer is *that*. If so, you'd be right – a correct gap fill would be *that*. However, *that* is not one of the options given, so you have to choose a word that means the same as *that*. Which is it?

WRITING PART 1

Questions 1 – 5

Here are some sentences about the weather.
For each question, complete the second sentence so that it means the same as the first.
Use no more than three words.
Write only the missing words.
You may use this page for any rough work.

Example:

0   Ken doesn't really like hot weather.

        Ken is not fond _____ **hot weather.**

Answer: | **0** | *of* |

1   Where Ken lives, it started raining over an hour ago.

     Where Ken lives, it's been raining _____*for*_____ **over an hour.**

2   There is water all over Ken's balcony because of the rain.

     Ken's balcony has _____*got/become*_____ **wet from all the rain.**

3   Ken is standing on his balcony despite the rain.

     Ken is standing on his balcony even _____*though*_____ **it's raining.**

4   Last year, the wind broke one of Ken's windows.

     Last year, one of Ken's windows was _____*broken by*_____ **the wind.**

5   Ken discovered the broken window when he got home from work.

     Ken found _____*out*_____ **about the broken window when he got home from work.**

TIPS

Remember that in this part you only have to write one to three words to complete the sentences. In fact, four of the answers here only need one word to fill the gap. Question 4 needs two words because you have to use the passive voice.

WRITING PART 2

Question 6

You are having a party to celebrate your birthday and you want to invite your friend Polly.

Write an email to Polly. In your email, you should:

- invite Polly to come
- tell her when and where the party is
- say what sort of party it is.

Write **35–45 words**.

Students' own answers

WRITING PART 3

Write an answer to **one** of the questions (**7** or **8**) in this part.
Write your answer in about **100 words**.

Question 7

- This is part of a letter you receive from an English friend.

> *My favourite sport is hockey. I play at school and*
> *on Saturdays with a team in the village where*
> *I live. What's your favourite hobby or sport?*
> *Please tell me all about it.*

- Now write a **letter** to your friend.

Question 8

- Your English teacher has asked you to write a story.
- Your story must begin with this sentence:

  James looked at his watch and knew it was time to go.

- Write your **story**.

Students' own answers

TIPS

In this part, you have a choice about what to write. Read both questions before you decide which is better for you to choose. Whichever one you choose, remember to think about answers to the questions *what*, *why*, *where*, *when* and *who*.

For example, if you are going to write about your favourite sport, say what it is, where and how often you do it, how you play it and who you play it with.

If you decide to continue the story, before you start writing think about where James was going, why he was going there, who he was going with and who (if anybody) he was going to meet. Make some notes about these things before you start writing and don't forget to begin with the opening sentence that is given.

When you have finished, read through your work to check it.

LISTENING PART 1

Questions 1 – 7

There are seven questions in this part.
For each question, choose the correct answer **A**, **B** or **C**.

Example: What does the girl buy?

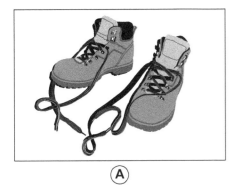

A

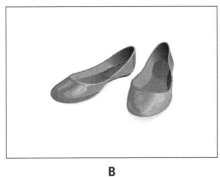

B

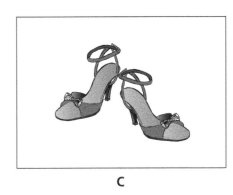

C

1   What is Jenny doing on Saturday?

A

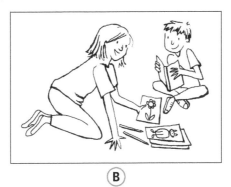

B

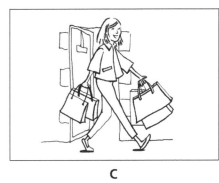

C

2   What film did Emma want to see?

A

B

C

3 What will listeners hear first on the radio show?

A

B

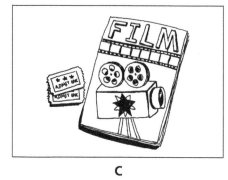

C

4 What new item of clothing is the boy wearing?

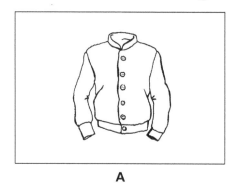

A

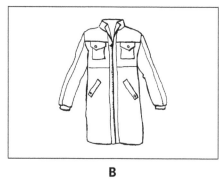

B

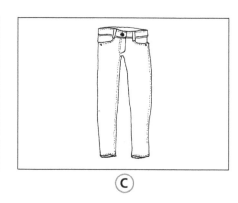

C

5 Where is the girl going on holiday?

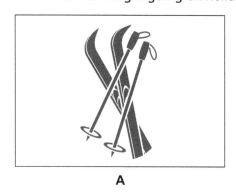

A

B

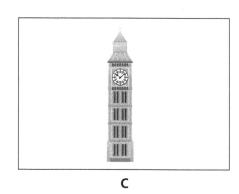

C

6   Where did Nick find the wallet?

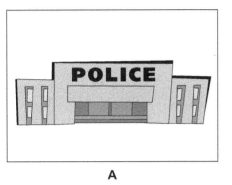

A

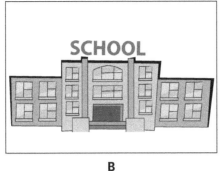

B

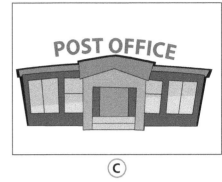

C

7   What are they going to do?

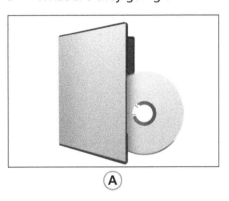

A

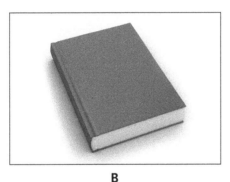

B

C

TIPS

As you will hear each part of the listening paper twice, don't worry if you don't get the answer on the first listening. For Part 1, which has seven different sections, write an answer immediately after each second listening. Don't leave any question unanswered. Don't think about any previous answer – give all your attention to the next section you will listen to.

For each section you will both hear and read the question. Each question begins with a question word, so make sure you know what you are listening for.

It's important to listen to the example. At the end, the girl says she will take <u>them</u>. How do you know she is talking about boots?

You should listen carefully for names that the speakers say. For example, in question 1, you will hear the names Penny, Jenny and Sally. They sound a bit similar, but you only want to know about <u>Jenny</u>'s plans.

LISTENING PART 2

Questions 8 – 13

You will hear an announcement about a new documentary. For each question, choose the correct answer **A**, **B** or **C**.

8 What kind of people will like the documentary?

  A people who are interested in space travel

  B people who like wildlife documentaries

  C people who like learning new facts

9 The new documentary series starting on TV tonight is about

  A different groups of people.

  B environments on and around the planet.

  C foreign countries and their landscapes.

10 The presenter of the documentary

  A knows a lot about the subject.

  B is an expert on British universities.

  C teaches people about space.

11 Why will the documentaries be easy to understand?

  A because the guests don't use complicated language

  B because the guests are experts on the topics

  C because the guests only explain the simple things

12 How do we know what space looks like?

  A Visitors to space have taken photos with a new kind of camera.

  B Scientists have used computers to make pictures of space.

  C Different forms of technology send us images of space.

13 What are viewers going to learn from the programme tonight?

  A information about the life of stars

  B scientists' opinions of other planets

  C lots of facts about Earth today

TIPS

Remember to use the time before you listen to read through the questions.

Before you listen to the announcement, you should underline the key information that you are looking for in the questions. For example, in question 8 you need to underline the last words of each option and listen to find what kind of people will like the documentary.

LISTENING PART 3

Questions 14 – 19

You will hear a man giving a walking tour of a castle.
For each question, fill in the missing information in the numbered space.

POWDERHAM CASTLE

Length of the tour: (14) ___*(about) 1/one hour*___

ROOMS:

Library: Contains collection of many (15) ___*antique*___ books

Dining room: Can seat more than (16) *100 / one hundred / a hundred* guests

Kitchen: Large wooden tables and a collection of (17) ___*knives*___

OUTSIDE:

Rose garden: Leads to a wooded area and a (18) ___*park*___ with deer

END OF TOUR:

Courtenay Gallery: Display of robes and a short (19) ___*documentary*___
to watch

TIPS

Use the short pause before you listen to read through the notes and try to predict the sort of information you need to put in the gaps.

For example, you know the answer to question 14 must be a time. How long do you expect a tour of a castle to be?

Remember that the answers you need are exactly as you hear them on the recording, and that you will need to write a number, a word or a short phrase in each gap. Don't write long answers.

LISTENING PART 4

Questions 20 – 25

Look at the six sentences for this part.
You will hear a conversation between a girl, Olivia, and a boy, Joe, about exams and tests.
Decide if each sentence is correct or incorrect.
If it is correct, choose the letter **A** for **YES**. If it is not correct, choose the letter **B** for **NO**.

		YES	NO
20	Joe believes he will get good marks in the coming test.	(A)	B
21	Olivia thinks that doing regular tests is more helpful than sitting exams.	A	(B)
22	Joe disagrees with Olivia's opinion about tests.	(A)	B
23	Olivia finds it hard to focus on both revision and homework.	(A)	B
24	Joe says schools keep the present system because it works.	(A)	B
25	Olivia thinks students should decide whether to do tests.	A	(B)

TIPS

In this part, you should make sure you understand the six sentences and who says what. Underline the names in the statements and key words to help you focus when you listen.

Question 20: What does Joe say that gives you the answer? Listen for something that means *will get good marks*.

Always circle an answer for every question on the question paper, even if you're just guessing. This will help you avoid missing answers when you are transferring them to the answer sheet at the end.

SPEAKING PART 1

2–3 minutes (3–4 minutes for a group of three)

Phase 1

This part is always the same. See page 30 of Test 1.

Phase 2
Interlocutor *(Select one or more questions from the list to ask each candidate. Use candidates' names throughout. Ask Candidate B first.)*

Do you like school? Why?/Why not?
What do you like doing at the weekend?
What is your favourite colour? Why do you like it?
Tell us what food you really like and what food you really dislike.
Thank you.

Introduction to Part 2
In the next part, you are going to talk to each other.

Students' own answers

TIPS

In Part 1, you only reply to simple questions from the examiner, so don't start asking your partner anything. It's a good idea to practise spelling your surname out loud before the exam.

Remember to give more than one word replies. For example, a good answer to the question: *Tell us what food you really like and what food you really dislike.* might be: *I really like pizza because it's tasty and you can choose many different things to put on it. I don't like red meat very much because it often has a lot of fat and it's not so healthy.*

Practice Test 2

SPEAKING PART 2

Suitable pet for an elderly person

Interlocutor
(Say to both candidates)

See pictures on page 171

I'm going to describe a situation to you.
An **elderly woman** lives alone and wants to get a pet for company. Talk together about the **different kind of pets** that would be **suitable** for an elderly person and then decide which would be the best.
Here is a picture with some ideas to help you.

I'll say that again.
An **elderly woman** lives alone and wants to get a pet for company. Talk together about the **different kind of pets** that would be **suitable** for an elderly person and then decide which would be the best.
All right? Talk together.

(Allow the candidates enough time to complete the task without intervention. Prompt only if necessary.)

Thank you.

Students' own answers

SPEAKING PART 3

3 minutes (4 minutes for a group of three)

Interlocutor *(Say to both candidates)*	Now, I'd like each of you to talk on your own about something. I'm going to give each of you a photograph of an **electronic gadget**.
See photo A on page 172	*(Candidate A)*, here is your photograph. Please show it to *(Candidate B)*, but I'd like you to talk about it. *(Candidate B)*, you just listen. I'll give you your photograph in a moment. *(Candidate A)*, please tell us what you can see in your photograph.
Candidate A *(If there is a need to intervene, prompts rather than direct questions should be used.)*	*(Approximately 1 minute)*
Interlocutor See photo B on page 172	Thank you. Now, *(Candidate B)*, here is your photograph. It also shows an **electronic gadget**. Please show it to *(Candidate A)* and tell us what you can see in the photograph.
Candidate B *(If there is a need to intervene, prompts rather than direct questions should be used.)*	*(Approximately 1 minute)*
Interlocutor	Thank you.

TIPS

In this part, you will speak by yourself for about a minute. When you talk about what you can see in your photograph, try to say as much as you can about it. For example, you can say what the photograph shows, what the object in the photograph looks like, what it is made of, where it is, and how you use it.

If you run out of things to talk about, you can say if you have a gadget like the one in the photograph and describe it. If you don't have that gadget, you can say if you would like to have it.

If you don't know the word for something you want to say, try to say it in another way. For example you could say *This is the thing that you use to look at the pictures and words on the computer.*

SPEAKING PART 4

3 minutes (3–4 minutes for a group of three)

Interlocutor *(Say to both candidates)*	Your photographs showed **electronic gadgets**. Now, I'd like you to talk together about **any electronic gadgets** that you **have** or that **you'd like to have**.

(Allow the candidates enough time to complete the task without intervention. Prompt only if necessary.)

Thank you. That's the end of the test. *Students' own answers*

TIPS

Remember that in this part you are talking with your partner, so show interest in what they say by commenting on it. Say things like, *That's interesting* or *I'd like one of those*, or ask questions about your partner's gadgets.

If your partner doesn't say much, try to include her or him by saying things like *What about you?* and *Do you have one of these at home?*

Practice Test 3

READING PART 1

Questions 1 – 5

Look at the text in each question.
What does it say?
Mark the correct letter **A**, **B** or **C**.

Example:

0

Special Sales Day tomorrow!

Buy one T-shirt, get one free!

Special offers from 10am to 3pm only!

Don't miss it!

A You can buy two T-shirts for the price of one.

B The shop is only open for three hours.

C It's easy to find the shop.

Answer: | 0 | A ■ | B ☐ | C ☐ |

1

Bob,
Dad phoned. He's going to be late tonight, so please take the dog for a walk when you get back from the gym. And don't forget to buy some cat food while you're out with the dog!
Your favourite sister!

What is Bob going to do first?

A take the dog for a walk

B go to the gym

C go to buy cat food

2

Zumba classes for teenagers!

Suitable for those who enjoy dancing and aerobics

It's fun and great exercise!

Come and give it a try – first lesson free.

Every day except Saturday and Sunday, 6pm–7pm.

A To see what Zumba is like, you can have a lesson at the weekend.

B To see if Zumba is suitable for you, you can have one lesson without paying.

C Zumba classes are available for all ages.

3

BALL GAMES ARE NOT ALLOWED IN THIS AREA OF THE PARK.

BICYCLES MUST BE PUSHED NOT RIDDEN.

KEEP DOGS ON A LEAD.

What should visitors to this area of the park do?

A play football here

B let their dogs run free

C get off their bikes

4

> **Wanted**
> Second-hand tennis racket
> For 10-year-old beginner
> Not pink please!
> Call Marcia 4563489

The advert says that

A you should call Marcia if you have a racket to sell.

B Marcia wants to sell a racket.

C Marcia wants a new tennis racket.

5

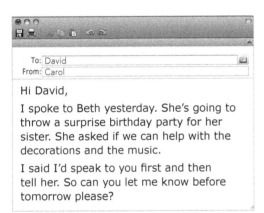

> To: David
> From: Carol
>
> Hi David,
> I spoke to Beth yesterday. She's going to throw a surprise birthday party for her sister. She asked if we can help with the decorations and the music.
> I said I'd speak to you first and then tell her. So can you let me know before tomorrow please?

What does Carol want David to do?

A organise the music for the party

B speak to Beth

C tell Carol if he can help with the party

READING PART 2

Questions 6 – 10

The teenagers below are all looking for a book to read.
On the opposite page, there are descriptions of eight different books for young people.
Decide which book would be the most suitable for the following teenagers.
For questions **6 – 10**, mark the correct letter (**A – H**).

6  Martha likes to read books about the problems between friends. In particular, she's looking for a book about a group of friends because she's having problems with her own friends.

H

7  Frank likes to read books that take him to different places while he's reading them. He likes light comedies and he's looking for a book with a bit of excitement in it.

F

8  Diane likes serious books with romance and heartache. She sometimes reads books that have happy endings, but now she's looking for a book that has a sad one.

D

9  Josh is reading books these days about problems kids have in their lives. He recently found out his best friend is very ill so he wants to read a story with a positive ending.

G

10  Caroline likes stories about relationships that have both humour and difficult moments. She wants to buy a book about unusual relationships.

E

Teen Books

A   *The Stranger Inside* is about a teenage boy who was in a car accident and can't remember who he is. He can't recognise his family or his girlfriend and they try to help him remember by taking him to places that were important in his life. This is an interesting book that sometimes makes us wonder how well we know ourselves.

B   When the new girl comes to town in *Falling To Pieces*, she quickly becomes popular. But she has a strange past that she wants to keep a secret. She runs into problems when she becomes close friends with a basketball teammate who also has a secret. When she finds out what it is, things become rather interesting.

C   *Together For Never* is a book about a teenage girl who falls in love with her handsome neighbour, Simon, who can't stand her. Sheila does everything she can to get Simon to notice her, but she fails every time. At one point, you wish Simon would just give in! The story has got lots of laughs.

D   *Hard Lesson* is a novel about Sophie, a teenage girl who becomes friends with Neil, a boy who has problems at school. Sophie tries to help Neil and defend him against kids who don't like him. She feels sorry for Neil and even falls in love with him. She's very upset when he is punished and has to leave school for good.

E   *Breaking Up* is a story about two teenagers who become friends after their relationship ends. Andy and Liz argued all the time while together, but become best friends when they split up. It's hard to tell what the funniest part of this book is – when they get on well or when they fight!

F   An action-filled story can be found in *The Girl Next Door*, set in Hawaii. When Sally Pickerton moves next door to Ralph Barns, things become interesting for Ralph. Not having many friends, Ralph is more than happy when Sally takes an interest in him. But after some crazy adventures, he may wish he'd never met her!

G   *Don't Give Up* tells the story of a young man with a serious illness who falls in love with his friend, Sarah. When Ryan's doctor tells him he has less than one year to live, Sarah helps him during his most difficult times. Their relationship shows that love sometimes cures all – even a serious illness.

H   This amusing story will have you laughing as you turn every page. *Love To Hate* tells the story of four girls who call themselves friends but are far from it. Each one of them tries to be the most popular at school, and each does cruel things to the others behind their backs. With friends like that, who needs enemies?

TIPS

Remember that the book must match what the person wants to read about exactly. It isn't the correct answer if only one thing matches. Make sure you read through the whole of the paragraphs A – H, before deciding on the match.

Question 6: The key thing Martha wants from a story is for it to be about <u>problems</u> between a <u>group</u> of friends. More than one book is about problems or difficulties in relationships, but only one is about problems in a group. Which one is it?

Question 8: The key words you should underline about Diane are *serious*, *romance*, *heartache* and *sad* (ending). You may think the correct match is G because it has the word *serious* twice and the people fall in love, but what about the ending? Is it sad?

READING PART 3

Questions 11 – 20

Look at the sentences below about a luxury hotel holiday and what it offers.
Read the text on the opposite page to decide if each sentence is correct or incorrect.
If it is correct, mark **A**.
If it is not correct, mark **B**.

11	Only takeaway food and snacks are served at the hotel.	A	**(B)**
12	The hotel is located on the coast.	**(A)**	B
13	This resort is only suitable for people who want action and adventure.	A	**(B)**
14	Nature lovers will probably get bored at this resort.	A	**(B)**
15	Some local villagers show people how to make things.	**(A)**	B
16	There are activities at the resort aimed at children.	**(A)**	B
17	You must take lessons before doing any water-based activities.	A	**(B)**
18	You need to reserve a place for kite-surfing beforehand.	**(A)**	B
19	Visitors may find that they cannot visit the lagoon.	**(A)**	B
20	You will probably find a room if you call the day before you arrive.	A	**(B)**

TIPS

You won't always find the same words in the questions and in the text. For example, the words *takeaway food* and *on the coast* are not near the beginning of the text. Which words in the text give you the answers for questions 11 and 12?

Some statements ask you to imagine the answer from what you read in the text. For example, question 14 says nature lovers will *probably* get bored. The text tells you what nature lovers can do at the resort. If you want to see lions or tigers, you will be disappointed, but can you imagine there is *probably* enough to interest nature lovers?

Question 17: Be careful to note any modal verbs in the statements. Here the word is *must*. Does the text say you *must* have lessons?

Question 19: Maybe you don't know the word *lagoon*. It doesn't matter if you don't because it tells you earlier in the text that it's a place where you can go bird pwatching. Anyway, you just need to find out if visitors may not always be able to go there.

The Pirate's Rest Hotel

The Hotel
Visit our luxury resort hotel! Come and enjoy the magnificent views, the sparkling blue sea and the wide range of exciting activities which will make your stay here a unique and memorable experience.

Food and Board
Our five-star hotel offers its guests great luxury and comfort. All the rooms are equipped with the softest beds and most beautiful antique furniture with original paintings on the walls. Our restaurant uses only the freshest local organic ingredients and all dishes, traditional and international, are prepared with love and care.

Peace and Relaxation
The resort offers many different activities for all tastes. It is situated in lush gardens on rolling hills, facing the sparkling blue sea. There is a beautiful sandy beach right in front of the hotel, whose waters are so clear you will think you are in heaven! For those who are looking for a relaxing holiday of swimming and sunbathing, this is the perfect place to be!

Adventure and Fun
If, on the other hand, you love nature and are interested in rare animals, there is also a magnificent lagoon nearby where you can go bird watching, or you can enjoy a peaceful walk on the paths and tracks in the forest close to the hotel. Off-road biking and trekking opportunities are also offered to sports enthusiasts.

For our guests who enjoy learning about traditional arts and crafts, there are woodwork and pottery classes in the neighbouring village. There, local people will be happy to share their skills and help visitors make their own souvenirs.

For more active guests, there are numerous fun activities, too. With a choice of tennis, horse-riding or scuba diving lessons, sports-lovers will never get bored in our resort. If you enjoy adventure, why not try rock climbing or white-water rafting nearby? And for our younger visitors, the theme park with the water slides will provide hours of endless fun!

Finally, don't forget the wide variety of water sports on offer, from canoeing on the lagoon to kite-surfing in the sea and the more traditional waterskiing and windsurfing, with instructors and trainers ready to help you at every step.

Please note: you must book these activities in advance as they are extremely popular. Also, access to the lagoon is not allowed at certain times of the year, as it is the nesting ground for birds and it is a protected area.

Reservations
As the demand for rooms in our resort is very high, we would advise you to book your dream holiday as early as possible.

More information
If you like what you see in this brochure and want further information regarding The Pirate's Rest Hotel, please contact us at: info@piratesresthotel.com or call us on 23407733456.

READING PART 4

Questions 21 – 25

Read the text and questions below.
For each question, mark the correct letter **A**, **B**, **C** or **D**.

School counselling – is it necessary?

In our grandparents' time, it was unthinkable. In our parents' time, it was unusual and nobody spoke openly about counselling. These days, more and more schools are asking for this service and it is considered a necessity for most. Why is that? What has changed in the last fifty years to have made counselling at schools so important?

'One reason is that we expect schools to do more to protect their pupils than we did in the past,' says school counsellor, Mike Hudson. 'Also, our society doesn't work as well as it should. Many parents are either under pressure of work or face the economic problems of unemployment, while children are under more and more pressure to do well at school. Many pupils feel they are pushed to their limits by their parents and teachers.'

Most school children face some kind of relationship problem at some stage with family members, teachers or other pupils, so it helps to have somebody to talk to. From the pupil's point of view, it is easier to talk to a counsellor in confidence rather than a family member or teacher. This solution is less embarrassing to adolescents, who are not obliged to face the person that they had problems with in the first place. They can calmly talk things through without arguments.

School counsellors advise not only students but also their teachers and parents, and offer other services as well, such as identifying learning disabilities or assisting parents and guardians to make the correct decisions about their children's education.

Counsellors can help students with problems ranging from the most serious, like a death in the family, to what an adult would consider really trivial or unimportant, like an argument with a friend.

In a society that is becoming more and more stressful, this service is providing children with a supportive way to express their fears and worries.

TIPS

Remember that it's important to read the whole text through before you try to answer any of the questions. That's why the questions come after the text.

If you don't know a word, for example, *counselling* or *counsellor*, don't worry. As you read through the text, you'll find out what a school counsellor is and does.

Question 21: Be careful to read the options carefully. It's easy to misread *unnecessary* as *necessary* in option A. In option D, there is the word *embarrassing*, and you find this word in the text, but does the writer believe that talking about school counselling is embarrassing?

Question 25: Remember that this question is about the meaning of the text as a whole. A counsellor may help teachers or parents, but which answer gives a more complete description of what a counsellor does?

21 What does the writer believe about school counselling?

   A It is unnecessary nowadays.

   B Our grandparents needed it more.

   C These days, we really need it.

   D It is embarrassing to talk about it.

22 Why does Mr Hudson think pupils need school counselling?

   A Parents and pupils are under too much pressure.

   B Pupils were protected more in the past.

   C Teachers don't care about their pupils.

   D Many parents are out of work.

23 Why do children prefer to talk to counsellors?

   A Children don't like their teachers.

   B Family members cannot keep secrets.

   C Children have no other friends.

   D Other people might get angry with them.

24 Who can school counsellors help?

   A students, parents or teachers who need help

   B students who have problems with homework

   C people who want to give a good education to their children

   D students, parents or teachers who want to improve

25 What might a school counsellor say about their job?

   A I help parents who have problems or are interested in finding good schools for their children.

   B I often give advice about smaller or bigger problems to anyone in the school community.

   C I do a job that used to be unimportant, but which is starting to become necessary.

   D I help teachers understand why their students behave the way they do.

READING PART 5

Questions 26 – 35

Read the text below and choose the correct word for each space.
For each question, mark the correct letter A, B, C or D.

Example:

0 **A** what   **B** where   **C** why   **D** who

Answer:

0	A	B	C	D

Hurricanes

Most people have heard of Hurricane Katrina, but **(0)** _____ exactly is a hurricane and what can we do to **(26)** _____ ourselves?

Hurricanes are enormous tropical storms which form over really warm oceans, but never very **(27)** _____ to the equator. What is interesting **(28)** _____ them is that the longer they stay at sea, the stronger they become, because they collect power from their contact with warm water. They can **(29)** _____ for over a week. The centre of the storm is called the 'eye' of the hurricane and it is the calmest part, but around the eye the **(30)** _____ strong winds, heavy rain and huge waves **(31)** _____ cause a lot of damage.

In areas where hurricanes happen, it is a good idea to have a first aid kit at all times, and to **(32)** _____ some cans of food and bottles of water in a safe place. You should also have a radio and extra batteries to listen to weather forecasts and the news.

(33) _____ there is a hurricane warning, get indoors immediately. During the hurricane, stay indoors and keep away from windows **(34)** _____ the strong winds may carry things that will break them and cause injuries. After the hurricane has passed, **(35)** _____ walking in flooded areas as the water might be dangerous. Try to help injured or trapped people, but do not risk your own safety. Do not drink tap water until you are told that it is clean.

26	**A** protect	**B** defend	**C** rescue	**D** advise
27	**A** nearby	**B** short	**C** close	**D** distant
28	**A** in	**B** to	**C** about	**D** for
29	**A** end	**B** last	**C** take	**D** run
30	**A** slightly	**B** extremely	**C** totally	**D** completely
31	**A** can	**B** should	**C** must	**D** would
32	**A** keep	**B** hold	**C** carry	**D** get
33	**A** Unless	**B** If	**C** Until	**D** While
34	**A** when	**B** although	**C** so	**D** as
35	**A** keep	**B** prevent	**C** start	**D** avoid

TIPS

As you read through the text for the first time without looking at the multiple-choice options, think about the words that can fill each gap. You can pencil in your own words if you want. If your word matches one of the options, it's probably correct.

If you look at the example, you'll see why it's important to read not just the words immediately before and after the gap. The next sentence answers the question (0); it tells you <u>what</u> hurricanes are.

Question 29: Remember that a good idea is to decide which options are *not* correct. Then you will have fewer options to choose from and your choice will be easier. Here, something cannot 'end' for over a week so you know that option A is not correct. Now you have only three options to choose from.

Question 34: When you read the text through the first time, you might have thought the answer was *because*. That word would be correct because the second part of the sentence gives a reason why you should keep away from windows. So you have to find the option that means the same as or something similar to *because*.

WRITING PART 1

Questions 1 – 5

Here are some sentences about safety in the home.
For each question, complete the second sentence so that it means the same as the first.
Use no more than three words.
Write only the missing words.
You may use this page for any rough work.

Example:

0   Don't leave young children alone at home.

You must _____ young children alone at home.

Answer: | **0** | *not leave* |

---

1   Always check that the cooker is off before going out.

If __*you go / you are going*__ out, you should always check that the cooker is off first.

2   'Don't take the radio into the bathroom. It's dangerous,' said Mum.

Mum told me _____*not to take*_____ the radio into the bathroom because it was dangerous.

3   Many accidents happen in the home because people are careless.

A _____*lot of*_____ accidents happen in the home because people are careless.

4   Many people get hurt because they do not pay attention to safety rules.

Many people hurt _____*themselves*_____ because they do not pay attention to safety rules.

5   Microwave ovens must be used with extreme care.

You should be extremely _____*careful*_____ when you use a microwave oven.

TIPS

Remember that you only write one to three words here. Don't forget that spelling is also very important in this task so check your spelling carefully when you have finished.

Question 2: You've probably got the right words to put in the gap, but is it *to not take* or *not to take*?

WRITING PART 2

Question 6

You are leaving for a week's holiday with your parents and you need to make arrangements for someone to take care of your pet.

Write a note to your Uncle Robert. In your note, you should:

- tell your uncle where you're going and how long you will be away

- ask him to take care of your pet

- thank him and say you will bring him something.

Write **35–45 words**.

Students' own answers

TIPS

Try to use your own words in your note. Don't just copy the words from the three bullet points and add a few words of your own. Try and use your own phrases. For example: *I'm not going to be here for...*, *look after...*, *look for a present for you while I'm on holiday.*

WRITING PART 3

Write an answer to **one** of the questions (**7** or **8**) in this part.
Write your answer in about **100 words**.

Question 7

- This is part of a letter you receive from an English friend.

> My family and I recently went to a carnival celebration. It was great fun. Do you have special festivals or celebrations like this in your country? Which one is your favourite? What happens on that day? Please tell me all about it.

- Now write a **letter** to your friend.

Question 8

- Your English teacher has asked you to write a story.
- This is the title for your story:

    The old bicycle

- Write your **story**.

Students' own answers

TIPS

If you choose question 7, remember to answer all the questions your friend asks.

Don't make up a festival or celebration – write about a real one that happens and that you have been to. This will be much easier for you to write about.

Remember to begin and end the letter properly.

If you choose question 8, you can write anything you like, but remember it must be a story, not just a description of an old bicycle.

Think about *who* the bicycle belonged to, *where* it was, and most importantly, *what* happened. Find a reason *why* the bicycle is interesting.

Remember that a story should have a beginning, a middle and an end.

LISTENING PART 1

Questions 1 – 7

There are seven questions in this part.
For each question, choose the correct answer **A**, **B** or **C**.

Example: Where does the boy want to go?

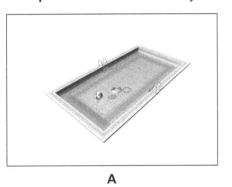

A

(B)

C

1 What time does the next bus pass?

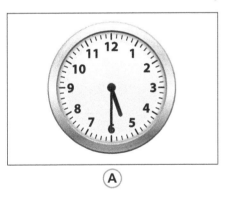

(A)

B

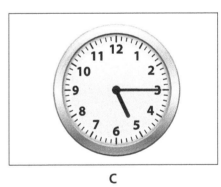

C

2 When was the last time the woman had her earrings on?

(A)

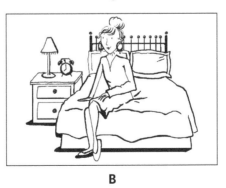

B

C

3 What is Peter's hobby?

A

B

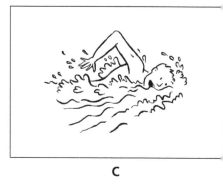

C

4 How will the father and son spend their day tomorrow?

A

B

C

5 What does the teacher tell the children to bring with them?

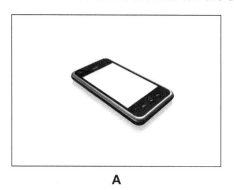

A

B

C

6   Which film are they going to watch?

A   B   C

7   What is Nick going to do next?

A   B   C

TIPS

Read the questions carefully. In the example, all the three places are mentioned, but the question asks where the boy _wants_ to go. You hear the words _swimming pool_ three times in the recording, but that doesn't mean it's the right answer.

Question 1: The key word in the question is _next_. You will hear all the three times shown, but here, as in many of the recordings in Part 1, the answer comes towards the end.

Question 6: The important thing here is that the question is about what the family _is going to_ watch finally. That may be different to what a particular family member _wants_ to watch.

LISTENING PART 2

Questions 8 – 13

You will hear part of an interview with a boy called Arthur Hobbs, who started a company which makes candles. For each question, choose the correct answer **A**, **B** or **C**.

8 What was Arthur's idea?

   A to raise money for charity by selling candles

   B to sell candles that smelt like flowers

   C to make candles with a different smell

9 What did his team ask him to do?

   A promise to give them back their money

   B give them pocket money

   C work very hard

10 How did Arthur feel about starting his business?

   A worried

   B excited

   C frightened

11 What did Arthur want to buy with the money from the candles?

   A cans of food

   B a bicycle

   C more candles

12 Arthur feels that his idea helps

   A all his family.

   B the environment.

   C shops sell more candles.

13 What are Arthur's future plans?

   A He wants to start a new company next year.

   B He doesn't want to go back to school.

   C He may start another business some time.

TIPS

Question 8: Although you will hear all three ideas mentioned, you need to listen carefully to hear which one Arthur thought of.

Question 10: You need to listen for an adjective that describes how Arthur felt. It must mean something very similar to one of the three options.

LISTENING PART 3

Questions 14 – 19

You will hear some information about a book.
For each question, fill in the missing information in the numbered space.

THE NEVERENDING STORY

Written by: Michael **(14)** _____Ende_____

Date of English translation: **(15)** _1983/nineteen eighty-three_

Bastian steals a: **(16)** _____strange_____ book

Bastian and Atreyu try to save: **(17)** _____the magic world_____ (called Fantastica)

Bastian loses his: **(18)** _____memory_____

Book is suitable for people over: **(19)** _____12/twelve_____

LISTENING PART 4

Questions 20 – 25

Look at the six sentences for this part.
You will hear a conversation between a boy, Stuart, and a girl, Erica, about a television programme called *Kids Can Cook*, a reality cooking show which teenagers take part in.
Decide if each sentence is correct or incorrect.
If it is correct, choose the letter **A** for **YES**. If it is not correct, choose the letter **B** for **NO**.

		YES	NO
20	Stuart got home in time to see the beginning of the show.	A	(B)
21	Erica says the kids had to cook something for famous vegetarians.	A	(B)
22	Stuart thinks the meal with fish should have won.	(A)	B
23	Stuart's mum always cooks things perfectly.	A	(B)
24	Stuart describes in detail how he makes a particular meal.	(A)	B
25	In the end, Erica believes Stuart has great cooking skills.	A	(B)

TIPS

Sometimes you will hear the exact words and phrases you read in the statements. For question 20 you'll hear *home in time*. What do you hear immediately before this phrase? Is it *got* or *didn't get*?

At other times you don't hear a key word in the statement. Question 21 has the word *vegetarians*. If you don't hear anything about a famous vegetarian – someone who doesn't eat any meat – then the statement cannot be correct.

Question 25: Listen for the way Erica speaks at the end. Her tone of voice will help you find the correct answer.

SPEAKING PART 1

2–3 minutes (3–4 minutes for a group of three)

Phase 1

This part is always the same. See page 30 of Test 1.

Phase 2
Interlocutor *(Select one or more questions from the list to ask each candidate. Use candidates' names throughout. Ask Candidate B first.)*

What's your favourite food? Why?

Where do you like eating when you go out? Why?

Who do you usually eat with?

Tell us what you usually eat for lunch.

Thank you.

Introduction to Part 2
In the next part, you are going to talk to each other.

Students' own answers

TIPS

If the examiner asks you where you live, you can say a little more than just the name of the town or city. For example: *I live in the centre of..., only about ten minutes' walk from here.*

There aren't any correct answers to questions about your favourite food or place to go out and eat. The examiner isn't going to judge you if you like fast food because it's not the healthiest food. Just say what's true for you.

SPEAKING PART 2

2–3 minutes (3 minutes for a group of three)

Best present for a teacher

Interlocutor
(Say to both candidates)

I'm going to describe a situation to you.
A school teacher is **retiring** at the end of the year. His students want to give him a **present**. Talk about the **different** presents his students could give him and then decide which present would be **best**.
Here is a picture with some ideas to help you.

See pictures on page 173

I'll say that again.
A school teacher is **retiring** at the end of the year. His students want to give him a **present**. Talk about the **different** presents his students could give him and then decide which present would be **best**.
All right? Talk together.

(Allow the candidates enough time to complete the task without intervention. Prompt only if necessary.)

Thank you.

Students' own answers

TIPS

When you're talking with your partner, the examiner will turn away. This is to encourage you to speak only with your partner and to speak to the examiner only if you need help.

Although the examiner asks you to decide on the best present, it doesn't matter if you don't agree or come to a conclusion. The important thing is that you talk about the different possibilities and why they are or are not suitable. Think about what the retiring teacher could do with each present. It's natural to use conditionals in this part, for example: *If they got him..., he would like it because he could....*

SPEAKING PART 3

3 minutes (4 minutes for a group of three)

Interlocutor *(Say to both candidates)*	Now, I'd like each of you to talk on your own about something. I'm going to give each of you a photograph of people **working on a farm**.
See photo A on page 174	*(Candidate A)*, here is your photograph. Please show it to *(Candidate B)*, but I'd like you to talk about it. *(Candidate B)*, you just listen. I'll give you your photograph in a moment. *(Candidate A)*, please tell us what you can see in your photograph.
Candidate A *(If there is a need to intervene, prompts rather than direct questions should be used.)*	*(Approximately 1 minute)*
Interlocutor See photo B on page 174	Thank you. Now, *(Candidate B)*, here is your photograph. It also shows people **working on a farm**. Please show it to *(Candidate A)* and tell us what you can see in the photograph.
Candidate B *(If there is a need to intervene, prompts rather than direct questions should be used.)*	*(Approximately 1 minute)*
Interlocutor	Thank you.

TIPS

Remember that in this part you and your partner each speak alone. You will be able to look at your partner's photo, but you shouldn't say anything about it, even if your partner gets stuck and can't think of anything to say.

When you have your photo, you only need to describe what you see – the person, where he/she is and what he/she is doing. Try to use a variety of language, for example, *In the centre, I can see ...*, *Over here there's a...*, *In the bottom right corner, we have a ...* .

SPEAKING PART 4

3 minutes (3–4 minutes for a group of three)

Interlocutor *(Say to both candidates)*	Your photographs showed people **working on a farm**. Now, I'd like you to talk together about the things **you would enjoy** on a farm and the things **you** might **find difficult** if you lived on a farm.

(Allow the candidates enough time to complete the task without intervention. Prompt only if necessary.)

Thank you. That's the end of the test.

Students' own answers

TIPS

Now you and your partner are talking together again, so remember you should take turns to speak and make comments on what your partner says.

Ask questions and use your imagination. If you don't live and work on a farm and have never been to one, you can still imagine what you would enjoy and what might be difficult about it. You have already seen two photos of people working on a farm, so you can imagine what that sort of life might be like.

You could talk about being in the open air, close to nature and being physically active as well as having to get up early and being far from other people. There's a lot to talk about.

READING PART 1

Questions 1 – 5

Look at the text in each question.
What does it say?
Mark the correct letter **A**, **B** or **C**.

Example:

0

> Hi Mum!
> London's amazing! We saw Big Ben today. There was a huge queue at the London Eye even though it had just rained. We'd already spent too much on lunch so we couldn't afford to go on it.
> Oh, well, next time!
> Pedro xxxx

Pedro says he didn't go on the London Eye

A because he didn't have enough money.

B because he didn't want to wait.

C because of the weather.

Answer:

| 0 | **A** ▬ | **B** ▭ | **C** ▭ |

1

> Ben,
>
> Thanks for remembering to take out the rubbish! Don't make lunch when you get back. It's Mum's birthday so we're eating out! Remember to buy her some flowers! See you after football!
>
> Katie

What does Katie remind Ben to do?

A to cook

B to empty the bin

C to bring a present

2

New offer till 1st September

Bring us your old sunglasses – get two new pairs 20% off

A In September, two pairs of sunglasses cost only 20% of the original price.

B Before September, you don't need to give your old sunglasses to get the offer.

C In August, you can recycle your old sunglasses to get two pairs of sunglasses more cheaply.

3

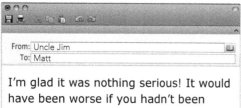

From: Uncle Jim
To: Matt

I'm glad it was nothing serious! It would have been worse if you hadn't been wearing your helmet. Check the tyres before you go next time! And go mountain biking when it's sunny and dry!

Why did Matt have an accident?

A He chose the wrong day to go cycling.

B He forgot to buy a new part for his bicycle.

C He didn't have the right protection.

4

Weekend Surfing!
Three-hour surfing lesson each day by qualified instructors

Course includes:

surfboard and wetsuit

two-hour free use of all equipment after lessons

beach picnics (July – August, large groups only)

A You must use your own surfboard on the course.

B You can continue practising after the lesson without paying extra.

C You are offered food when there aren't many people.

5

Monday, 3rd May

Mary might have to resit some of her exams this term. Please call the school secretary to arrange a meeting. I'm away and won't be back before Thursday this week.

With regards,

Mr Jones

A Mary's parents can't see the teacher on Wednesday.

B The school secretary will phone Mary's parents after Thursday.

C This term, Mary is going to fail most of the school subjects.

READING PART 2

Questions 6 – 10

The teenagers below are all looking for a TV programme to watch.
On the opposite page there are descriptions of eight different TV programmes for young people.
Decide which TV programme would be the most suitable for the following teenagers.
For questions **6 – 10**, mark the correct letter (**A – H**).

---

6  James would like to watch a TV programme that's full of action and mystery, but doesn't include fighting. He also likes solving puzzles and playing the guitar.

C

7  Tina loves learning about different cities around the world, but she finds documentaries rather boring. She'd like to know more about how life might be after leaving school.

H

8  Roberto spends most of his time doing sports and reading about space. He prefers watching films in their original language, but he's not a fan of romantic or adventure stories.

E

9  Trevor doesn't like science fiction and he's bored with TV detective series. When he feels like watching television, he prefers action with a cheerful storyline.

G

10  Jess is interested in music and enjoys reading science fiction stories about strange creatures. She trains hard at football practice after school, so she prefers to relax and watch something funny at the weekend.

B

TV programmes

A   **The Queen Of Ice** is intense and combines drama and romance. It's on every Tuesday and Thursday. If you like figure-skating and a good love story, then don't miss a single episode. Lizzie is fighting to win the championship, but also to keep Gordon, her boyfriend. Will Mandy take both the cup and Gordon away from her?

B   **Hunt Them Down!** Bob and Ben are twins who wake up one day to find a scary alien from Mars having breakfast in their kitchen! Don't worry: they know how to get rid of it (but more are on their way). Tune in every Sunday evening to watch the funny adventures of the best anti-alien duo!

C   **Teenage Mind** Nobody knew Spencer until the day he helped the police catch a bank robber. Now he's the most popular student in the school! Watch how this intelligent teenage detective uses his brains to solve difficult mysteries. Use your own detective skills and help Spencer find the solution to the mystery every Saturday evening.

D   **Not So Easy** is a new TV documentary focusing on the life of four teenagers who live in very different countries. Do you have problems at home, at school or with your friends and don't know how to face them? So do the teenagers in this programme. Why don't you watch an episode to see how others your age deal with difficult situations?

E   **Welcome To Mars!** has thousands of fans around the world. It's about the first city built by humans on this actually very unwelcoming planet. It's an amazing story not only because of the realistic-looking sets, but also because of the special effects. It's filmed in Japanese with English subtitles, so it's good practice for anyone learning Japanese.

F   **Flying Swords** has twelve episodes full of knights and princesses, dwarves, monsters and wizards. Watch the battles between them, but don't be surprised if the good guys get hurt. The special effects and the theme song have won many awards. There's an episode on the first Saturday of each month.

G   You might think that it's a girlie programme, but you're wrong. Even though it's a love story, **Don't Break My Heart** has lots of action and mystery with plenty of funny moments. The plot is so entertaining that you'll want to watch all of the fifteen episodes. If I were you, I wouldn't miss a single one!

H   If you're into rock music and dancing, don't miss **Rocking Our Class**. It's as good as any musical you've seen at the cinema, or on stage. The main characters study at an art college in London. So, you'll see what it's like to live in a big city and study at university. Don't forget! Every Friday, we'll rock you!

READING PART 3

Questions 11 – 20

Look at the sentences below about a practical recycling guide for kids to use at home.
Read the text on the opposite page to decide if each sentence is correct or incorrect.
If it is correct, mark **A**.
If it is not correct, mark **B**.

11	People often begin a recycling plan by putting a recycling bin in the kitchen.	(A)	B
12	Parents are the only people that can help with recycling plans.	A	(B)
13	Recycling bins should be placed in other rooms in the home.	(A)	B
14	Some items should be used again instead of being recycled.	(A)	B
15	You must store food in items that can't be recycled.	A	(B)
16	Giving recycled items to other people might encourage them to recycle.	(A)	B
17	The main reason to clean items for recycling is to keep bins clean.	A	(B)
18	You should use soap to clean recycled items.	A	(B)
19	Workers in recycling centres can use their time better if they don't have to clean items.	(A)	B
20	Recycling is something that must become a regular routine.	(A)	B

Practical recycling

If your home is like most others, you've probably got a recycling bin in your kitchen. Good for you! That's the first step to recycling. But there are other things that everyone in the house, both parents and kids, can do to make recycling work better.

First, what kinds of rubbish bins are in the other rooms of your house? What about in your bedroom? You've probably just got one rubbish bin where everything goes. But it's a good idea to place a special bin for recycling paper. Then, when it gets full, you can empty it into a larger recycling bin in the kitchen. You can also put a small recycling bin in the bathroom for any paper items that get thrown away there.

Before you throw an item into the recycling bin, stop and think for a minute. Can you use that item again? Take plastic items that contain yoghurt, for example. After eating what's in them, you can clean them and store them in a cupboard, and later you can use them for storing another food item. You can do the same with glass jars, too. You can even give these items to your neighbours with biscuits or a nice gift inside and, at the same time, you can share your recycling advice.

If you decide to put an item in the recycling bin, it's very important to follow this method. If it had food or drink in it, you must be sure to clean it before you put it in the recycling bin. You might be wondering why you must clean it first. Before any item can be recycled, it must be cleaned to get rid of anything that's not part of it. It can't be recycled with food still in it. You should place the item under running water for a few seconds to clean it. This saves time for the workers in the recycling centre. Then they can use their time doing more important work.

The last thing to remember is – don't give up! You mustn't just do recycling for a month and then return to your old habits. You can also continue to find other ways to recycle. This guide contains a few of the basic steps, but if you read more about it, you'll find that there are many more things you can do. So make recycling your new habit, and get others involved as well!

READING PART 4

Questions 21 – 25

Read the text and questions below.
For each question, mark the correct letter **A**, **B**, **C** or **D**.

The Holi festival

Thirteen-year-old Lydia Dawson talks about an unusual festival

Home again after two weeks in India! My parents are asleep, exhausted from the long flight. My sister is chatting with her boyfriend and I feel wide awake. I keep thinking of the cows in the streets of Delhi, the temples and the bazaars. But I'm just going to write about Holi, the Festival of Colours in Barsana! It was unbelievable!

We had to go there by bus from Delhi because Dad didn't want to drive. Both he and Mum weren't feeling well because it was so hot. My sister and I didn't mind the heat or the constant stops. It was so interesting to watch passengers getting on and off the bus! Some of them had big old suitcases and I saw a man carrying a monkey in a box! I never wanted the trip to end.

My favourite memory of India!

We finally got to Barsana, left our luggage at the hotel and went straight out! Hundreds or maybe thousands of people were in the street throwing *gulal*, the colourful powder, in the air! At first, I was worried about my new T-shirt, but I quickly forgot about it! I found a man selling *gulal* and asked for a bag. He explained that it was a bit expensive because it was made of flowers. I didn't expect it to smell so nice! It was like opening a bag of perfume!

When I'd thrown all my *gulal* at my sister and my parents, I started clicking away with my camera. The best photos were of children shooting coloured water with water pistols. They went after their parents and other adults, even tourists, but nobody got annoyed. Everybody was laughing and enjoying themselves. It felt like we were all one family without any differences between us. We weren't only celebrating the beginning of spring; we were celebrating life and how colourful it can be! Why don't we have festivals like this here in Ireland? We should, shouldn't we?

21 Why did Lydia write this text?

    A to tell readers what her family is doing

    B to let her friends know that she's returned from her trip

    C to describe an experience she had during the trip

    D to explain why she can't go to sleep

22 What does Lydia say about the bus trip?

    A Not everyone in her family enjoyed the trip.

    B It ended quickly because the bus was fast and comfortable.

    C She wanted to get off the bus at every stop.

    D She wanted to get to Barsana as soon as possible.

23 What did Lydia think about the colourful *gulal*?

    A She thought that it was quite expensive.

    B She didn't like it because it would destroy her clothes.

    C She was surprised that so many people were throwing it.

    D She was surprised that it smelt nice.

24 Lydia enjoyed the Holi festival because

    A children could behave badly.

    B people acted as if they were all the same.

    C it doesn't happen in Ireland.

    D it was the start of spring.

25 What advice might Lydia give to someone travelling to Barsana for the Holi festival?

    A Don't travel there by bus because it takes too long.

    B Don't take a camera with you or the *gulal* will destroy it.

    C Wear old clothes because you will get *gulal* all over you!

    D Avoid children with water pistols – they're very annoying!

READING PART 5

Questions 26 – 35

Read the text below and choose the correct word for each space.
For each question, mark the correct letter **A**, **B**, **C** or **D**.

Example:

0 A good   **B** better   **C** best   **D** well

Answer:

0	A	B	C	D
	☐	☐	▬	☐

The Coco Taxi

For many tourists, the **(0)** _____ way to see a big city is **(26)** _____ foot. It's not only better than taking the underground or some **(27)** _____ kind of public transport, but it's also better for the environment. However, in some cities around the world **(28)** _____ are quite unusual ways of getting around. Take, for instance, the coco taxi in Havana, Cuba. The streets of Havana are full of these funny little vehicles. **(29)** _____ they're small in size, you'll be surprised at how fast they can go.

A coco taxi is basically a three-wheeled vehicle, similar to a small motorbike, **(30)** _____ by a round plastic structure. It looks **(31)** _____ a huge yellow coconut, which is why locals call it 'coco taxi'. There's only **(32)** _____ for two people to sit at the back, while the driver sits in the front. They're not as cheap **(33)** _____ the regular taxis but they're more fun!

Even though the yellow coco taxis are a symbol of the Cuban capital, not everyone can use them. Only tourists are **(34)** _____ to ride in them, and local Cubans use the ordinary black taxis. Coco taxis have been zooming around Havana since 1998 and now every visitor sees a ride in one as something they must **(35)** _____ on their trip to Havana.

26	**A** by	**B** at	**C** in	**D** on
27	**A** other	**B** another	**C** all	**D** each
28	**A** they	**B** these	**C** there	**D** their
29	**A** Although	**B** Despite	**C** However	**D** Even
30	**A** closed	**B** covered	**C** built	**D** made
31	**A** similar	**B** as	**C** like	**D** same
32	**A** gap	**B** area	**C** place	**D** room
33	**A** that	**B** than	**C** so	**D** as
34	**A** let	**B** allowed	**C** made	**D** provided
35	**A** make	**B** get	**C** do	**D** go

WRITING PART 1

Questions 1 – 5

Here are some sentences about a girl who plays the drums.
For each question, complete the second sentence so that it means the same as the first.
Use no more than three words.
Write only the missing words.
You may use this page for any rough work.

Example:

0   Alice hasn't got her own drums because they're too expensive.

Drums aren't _____ **for Alice to get her own.**

Answer: | **0** | *cheap enough* |

---

1   When Alice was younger, she played the guitar, but now she plays the drums.

Alice used _____ *to play* _____ **the guitar, but now she plays the drums.**

2   Alice also plays the piano, but not as well as the drums.

Alice plays the drums _____ *better than* _____ **she plays the piano.**

3   Alice would like to practise more, but she doesn't have a drum kit.

If Alice _____ *had* _____ **a drum kit, she would practise more.**

4   'Take your drumsticks with you!' Alice's mum says to her before every lesson.

Before every lesson, Alice's mum reminds her _____ *to take* _____ **her drumsticks with her.**

5   Alice has to practise for a school concert in June.

After June, Alice _____ *doesn't have/need / won't have/need* _____ **to practise for the school concert.**

WRITING PART 2

Question 6

You are on holiday with your parents in another country.

Write a postcard to your friend. In your postcard, you should:

- tell your friend what the weather is like
- describe what you have done so far
- say what you are going to do and how you feel about your holiday.

Write **35–45 words**.

Students' own answers

WRITING PART 3

Write an answer to **one** of the questions (**7** or **8**) in this part.
Write your answer in about **100 words**.

Question 7

- This is part of a letter you receive from an English friend.

> *I'm going to my ten-year-old cousin's birthday party next weekend and I want to buy a present for him. What do you think I should give him? How can I find out what he wants without asking him?*

- Now write a **letter** to your friend.

Question 8

- Your English teacher has asked you to write a story.
- Your story must begin with this sentence:

    Our holiday started out very well, but it didn't end that way.

- Write your **story**.

Students' own answers

LISTENING PART 1

Questions 1 – 7

There are seven questions in this part.
For each question, choose the correct answer **A**, **B** or **C**.

Example: What time are the boys meeting?

A

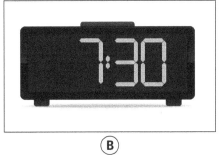

Ⓑ

C

1 How is the girl getting to school?

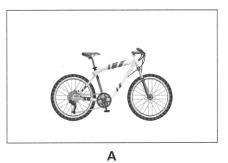

A

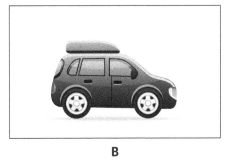

B

Ⓒ

2 What did the girl forget?

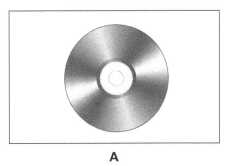

A

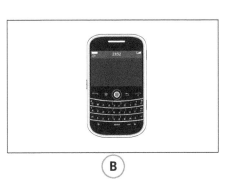

Ⓑ

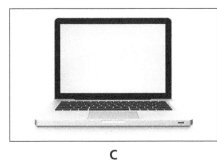

C

3 What was the final score?

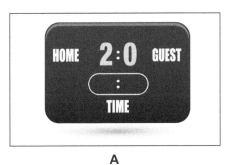

A

Ⓑ

C

4 What are they going to play?

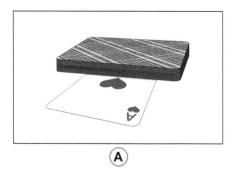

A

B

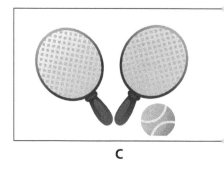

C

5 Where will the boy do the English course?

A

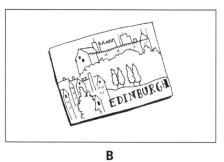

B

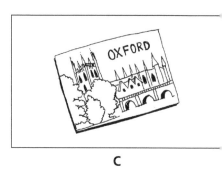

C

6 What does the boy need help with?

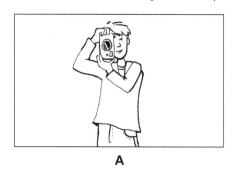

A

B

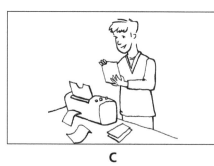

C

7 What is the girl going to wear to the party?

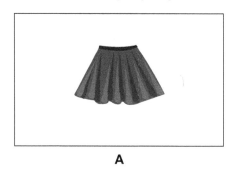

A

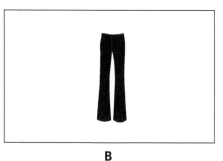

B

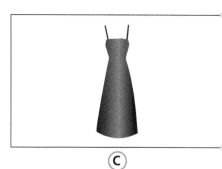

C

LISTENING PART 2

Questions 8 – 13

You will hear a school reporter interviewing Paul Reynolds, a journalist, who wrote an article on unusual or dangerous jobs. For each question, choose the correct answer **A, B** or **C**.

8 Greetings card writers sometimes

   A write the message for the card.

   B write the message and draw the picture.

   C write a message for the front of the card.

9 Writing greetings cards is

   A fun because some cards are funny.

   B challenging because the card should be original.

   C easy because there isn't much to write.

10 Paul thinks that greetings card writers

   A get paid well for what they do.

   B earn too much money.

   C could sell a card for hundreds of euros.

11 What is the most dangerous thing about being a window cleaner?

   A They have to work when the weather is bad.

   B Sometimes they work without protection.

   C In some places, they work at great heights.

12 Paul says that to become a window cleaner you need

   A strength and fitness.

   B to become a climber.

   C height.

13 When do window cleaners have to stop working?

   A early in the afternoon

   B when the sun is very bright

   C at sunset

LISTENING `PART 3`

Questions 14 – 19

You will hear a weather report on the radio.
For each question, fill in the missing information in the numbered space.

WEATHER FORECAST

Thursday

All day: cloudy

Daytime temperatures:

Northern England: **(14)** _____ *below* _____ 12°C

South-west England: up to **(15)** _____ *15/fifteen* _____ °C

Friday

Morning: heavy **(16)** _____ *rain* _____

Evening: dry and **(17)** _____ *(quite) cold* _____

Saturday

Warm and sunny

Sunday

Strong north **(18)** _____ *wind(s)* _____

Travelling conditions could be: **(19)** _____ *dangerous* _____

LISTENING PART 4

Questions 20 – 25

Look at the six sentences for this part.
You will hear a conversation between a girl, Rebecca, and a boy, Steve, who live in a small town.
Decide if each sentence is correct or incorrect.
If it is correct, choose the letter **A** for **YES**. If it is not correct, choose the letter **B** for **NO**.

		YES	NO
20	Steve's mother was ill at the weekend.	A	(B)
21	Rebecca likes playing some computer games.	(A)	B
22	Steve thinks that there is a good sports centre in Amersham.	A	(B)
23	Rebecca suggests riding their bikes if the weather is suitable.	(A)	B
24	Steve asks Rebecca to take some books when they go out.	A	(B)
25	Steve and Rebecca are meeting at the park.	A	(B)

SPEAKING PART 1

2–3 minutes (3–4 minutes for a group of three)

Phase 1

This part is always the same. See page 30 of Test 1.

Phase 2
Interlocutor *(Select one or more questions from the list to ask each candidate. Use candidates' names throughout. Ask Candidate B first.)*

Have you or your friends got any pets? Tell us about a pet you know.
What is your favourite kind of pet? What do you like about it?
Tell us about a pet you would like to have.
Are there any animals you think should not be pets? Which ones? Why?
Thank you.

Introduction to Part 2
In the next part, you are going to talk to each other.

Students' own answers

SPEAKING PART 2

2–3 minutes (3 minutes for a group of three)

Arrangements for a party

Interlocutor
(Say to both candidates)

I'm going to describe a situation to you.
A girl is going to celebrate her **birthday** at her house this weekend. She is going to **invite her friends** from school. Talk together about the different things the girl has to **organise** and decide which three are the **most important**.

See pictures on page 175

Here is a picture with some ideas to help you.

I'll say that again.
A girl is going to celebrate her **birthday** at her house this weekend. She is going to **invite her friends** from school. Talk together about the different things the girl has to **organise** and decide which three are the **most important**.
All right? Talk together.

(Allow the candidates enough time to complete the task without intervention. Prompt only if necessary.)

Thank you.

Students' own answers

SPEAKING PART 3

3 minutes (4 minutes for a group of three)

Family celebration

Interlocutor *(Say to both candidates)*	Now, I'd like each of you to talk on your own about something. I'm going to give each of you a photograph of **a family celebrating a special occasion.**
See photo A on page 176	*(Candidate A)*, here is your photograph. Please show it to *(Candidate B)*, but I'd like you to talk about it. *(Candidate B)*, you just listen. I'll give you your photograph in a moment. *(Candidate A)*, please tell us what you can see in your photograph.
Candidate A *(If there is a need to intervene, prompts rather than direct questions should be used.)*	*(Approximately 1 minute)*
Interlocutor See photo B on page 176	Thank you. Now, *(Candidate B)*, here is your photograph. It also shows **a family celebrating a special occasion**. Please show it to *(Candidate A)* and tell us what you can see in the photograph.
Candidate B *(If there is a need to intervene, prompts rather than direct questions should be used.)*	*(Approximately 1 minute)*
Interlocutor	Thank you.

SPEAKING PART 4

3 minutes (3–4 minutes for a group of three)

Interlocutor *(Say to both candidates)*	Your photographs showed **families celebrating a special occasion**. Now, I'd like you to talk together about how **you** usually celebrate with **your family** and describe the **best** family celebration you have **ever** had.

(Allow the candidates enough time to complete the task without intervention. Prompt only if necessary.)

Thank you. That's the end of the test.

Students' own answers

Practice Test 5

READING PART 1

Questions 1 – 5

Look at the text in each question.
What does it say?
Mark the correct letter **A**, **B** or **C**.

Example:

0

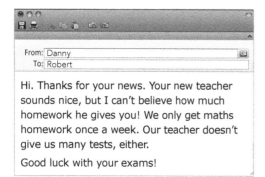

From: Danny
To: Robert

Hi. Thanks for your news. Your new teacher sounds nice, but I can't believe how much homework he gives you! We only get maths homework once a week. Our teacher doesn't give us many tests, either.

Good luck with your exams!

What does Danny do in his email?

A   He gives his opinion.

B   He asks about the maths teacher.

C   He tells Robert about his exam.

Answer:

1

Dance Class

Today's dance practice is not on because the teacher is off sick. Next practice at usual time next week.

A   The teacher is not available next week.

B   This week, the dance practice is on at a different time.

C   There is no dance practice this week.

2

Please keep your receipt.

Refund or exchange available up to 20 days after you buy clothes. Show your receipt when returning any items.

A   You must wait for twenty days before you bring anything back here.

B   Everyone can get their money back for clothes they bought here.

C   If you want to take something back, you must prove when you bought it.

3

All passengers please note:
Remember to put your
ticket in the machine at
the platform gate.

Where is this sign?

A   at an airport

B   at a railway station

C   on a bus

4

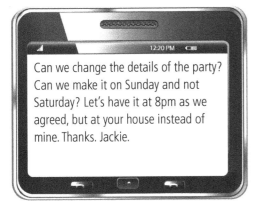

Can we change the details of the party?
Can we make it on Sunday and not
Saturday? Let's have it at 8pm as we
agreed, but at your house instead of
mine. Thanks. Jackie.

What does Jackie want to do?

A   have the party on another day and in another
place

B   change the place and the time of the party

C   have the party on a different weekend

5

FOR SALE
Mountain bike
Three years old
In great condition – new tyres and brakes.
Phone Fred: 8723624 to arrange collection.

The advert says the bike

A   may need some repairs.

B   is ready for a customer to pick up.

C   is only suitable for very young cyclists.

READING PART 2

Questions 6 – 10

The teenagers below are all interested in going to a museum or a gallery.
On the opposite page, there are descriptions of eight museums and galleries.
Decide which museum or gallery would be the most suitable for the following teenagers.
For questions **6 – 10**, mark the correct letter (**A – H**).

6

Martin enjoys learning about technology and reading about inventions. He also likes to try things out to understand how they work, as well as looking at pictures and models of them.

C

7

Martha loves drawing and she wants to learn how to make her own clothes. She collects photos of different designs and she'd also like to find an unusual costume to wear to a fancy dress party.

F

8

Tom would like to study art although he isn't very interested in classical paintings. He has visited quite a few galleries of all kinds and he is particularly keen on modern sculpture.

E

9

Jane really likes looking at old pictures by the famous painters of the past. She also enjoys reading and would like to find out more about the history of art.

H

10

Ken has visited ancient sites in different parts of the world with his parents. He is more interested in learning about how people lived a long time ago than in wars people fought.

B

Museums and galleries

A The **Science Experiment** is for people who love science and want to learn about the history of scientific discovery. We have the original designs and documents from some of the greatest scientists. There is a scientist's laboratory with all the equipment a scientist would have used 100 years ago. But you mustn't touch anything – the equipment and papers are all original and very valuable.

B The **World Museum of the Past** has a large collection of items which help us to understand life in years gone by. The main room contains things which archaeologists believe came from homes in the ancient world. You can read about the lives of ordinary people and see a model of a kitchen, a bedroom and public baths exactly as they were thousands of years ago.

C The **Grovehampton Museum** contains a huge number of machines, inventions and items from the past, which take visitors on a journey through the history of technology. Visitors can learn to operate some of the exhibits, and can pick up and touch models of the inventions like the first telephone or an early computer. In the gift shop, there are many books, diagrams and CDs on sale which explain everything you want to know about the things in the exhibition.

D The **House of Words and Pictures** is a gallery, a museum, a bookshop and a café! On display, you will find books on art, fashion, technology, history – you can even find books about books! The HoW&P has some of the oldest books in the world, and there is an exhibition about famous writers with some of the desks and pens they used in the past. One room is a model of the famous room where a great French writer wrote his books.

E The **Art of Stone** is an exhibition at the Baronstone Museum of Sculpture. Visitors will see a range of statues from all over the world by some of the most famous sculptors today. Students of art will be interested to learn that the museum shows a short film about the different styles and types of sculpture on display every fifteen minutes.

F This month at the **Modern Museum of London** is definitely for followers of fashion. There are hundreds of dresses, coats and jackets, as well as shoes, bags and hats. The museum shows you clothes from the last 300 years and demonstrates how fashion and design have developed over the centuries. You can try on some of the clothes and our shop sells copies of some of the things on display.

G The **Novell Picture Gallery** has a new exhibition of pictures, from the beginning of photography to the present day. There are many photographs from the past, and visitors are offered a view of the world of their grandparents – or even earlier! They can see how people lived, what they wore and much more. This is a great exhibition for students of history as well as those interested in the art of photography. The collection includes some examples of the images created by the greatest photographers. There is also a small display of cameras from the nineteenth and twentieth centuries.

H The **Southbury Gallery** is a private collection of art from the last 1,000 years. The paintings hanging on our walls include some of the most important works in the development of art in Europe, and the museum presents an interesting journey through the history of painting up to the nineteenth century. Our gift shop has a lot of books and postcards to choose from.

READING PART 3

Questions 11 – 20

Look at the sentences below about a website for summer jobs for teenagers.
Read the text on the opposite page to decide if each sentence is correct or incorrect.
If it is correct, mark **A**.
If it is not correct, mark **B**.

11	The website offers permanent jobs.	A	**(B)**
12	You can find a great holiday on this website.	A	**(B)**
13	The site is connected to other, similar sites.	**(A)**	B
14	You can write something about yourself on the website.	**(A)**	B
15	The website is only for people who want to work for big companies.	A	**(B)**
16	There are jobs available for people who do not want to leave home.	**(A)**	B
17	Summer Work Finder will contact companies in your area for you.	A	**(B)**
18	Teenagers will be in charge of groups of children at summer camps.	A	**(B)**
19	All students need permission from their parents to work on a farm.	A	**(B)**
20	A summer job could be a good way to see the world.	**(A)**	B

Summer work finder

Welcome to www.summerworkfinder.co.uk! If you are looking for something interesting to do just for a few weeks in the summer, you're in the right place. Lots of young people spend their summer holidays working, and for lots of different reasons. You might want to earn some money, or you might want to travel, or perhaps you just want a new experience helping others during the summer break. Whatever your reason, this page will tell you everything you need to know about getting a job for this season.

Summer Work Finder will help you find exactly what you're looking for! We have advertisements for jobs from all over the country and we also have links to other websites with jobs for university students. You can even post an advertisement about yourself! Just write your CV and describe what sort of work you want, then wait for the offers to come!

There are lots of different jobs you could do. Most of you probably want a local job, for example, in a nearby shop or a café, or dog-walking. Some local companies employ students to do easy jobs while some of their staff are on holiday. Then your parents won't have to worry about you travelling away from home. Whatever you'd like to try, we'll put you in touch with people in your area who need young people to help out in the summer.

If you're an older student and you want to work away from home for a short working break in the countryside, you could choose to work in a summer camp or a community centre. They often need teenage assistants to help the staff who are responsible for organising activities for young children. You could even work outdoors picking fruit on a farm. However, remember that if you're under 18 and want to work away from home, you must have your parents' permission.

If you're at university and feel adventurous enough to travel abroad, we can tell you where to contact big organisations which help people in foreign countries. You might even travel to Africa or South America with them to work for a short time.

So whatever your interests are, you will find job offers to match them here. Just click on the links to discover a world of new opportunities!

READING PART 4

Questions 21 – 25

Read the text and questions below.
For each question, mark the correct letter **A**, **B**, **C** or **D**.

Making our home eco-friendly

Fourteen-year-old David Neilson describes what his family did to make their house eco-friendly.

A few months ago, our family decided to make our house eco-friendly. We had already done some things to prevent damage to the environment, such as replacing the old light bulbs with modern low-energy ones. This was a simple way to use less electricity in general. But we wanted to do even more.

First, we changed the way we heat our water. As we are a big family, we use a lot of hot water. We used to use a lot of electricity to keep heating it, but that wasted too much power and, of course, it cost too much. We put solar panels on the roof of our house. These have made a big difference. We don't have to worry about wasting electricity because they use sunlight to heat our water. This means our bills are much lower, too.

Next, we had new windows put in all the rooms. They are double windows, so this means we don't lose so much heat from the building. We put extra windows on the sides of our roof, too. These windows allow natural light to come into our rooms, so we don't have to use our electric lights as much. My parents employed people to put all these windows in. Before they started working, we had to cover all our furniture. The whole house was in a real mess for days! There were holes in the ceiling and it seemed like the work would never end. It was an interesting project to watch, but it was an expensive job for my parents to pay for. They believe it was worth it, though. Now we've got so much more natural light in our house that we don't need to turn on the lights so often.

Last of all, we've now got an electronic system to control the light switches. This system uses things which are called motion detectors. They notice when anyone enters or leaves a room. It might sound too scientific, but it's easy to understand. The system turns a light on when someone (or something – like our cat!) goes into a room. Then it switches the light off when they leave. We have them in all the rooms because we always used to forget to turn the lights off, especially my little sisters!

I'm glad we made these changes because they've made our home a warmer and brighter place. I think this is a brilliant idea for people who can afford to do it. The improvements may cost a lot, but they will save money after some time and help the environment, too.

21 Why has David written this text?

    A to describe how to build things

    B to explain a family project

    C to say how much energy things use

    D to talk about problems in the environment

22 What does David say about solar panels on the roof?

    A He wishes his house had more of them.

    B He thinks they waste too much energy.

    C He says they save money.

    D He believes they were expensive.

23 How does David feel about the new windows?

    A He is worried about the damage to the roof.

    B They are helpful for homes that don't have lights.

    C He liked the house better before they got them.

    D He believes they have made an improvement.

24 How did the motion detector change things?

    A The lights go on when someone makes a sound.

    B David doesn't forget to turn the light off as often as before.

    C David's sisters understand how it works.

    D Every light in the house works automatically now.

25 What might David's parents write about the project?

A
We really enjoyed our project. We liked learning how to put in solar panels, extra windows and motion detectors. We hope to learn how to use these things around the house soon.

B
The eco-friendly project was a good learning experience. It made everyone think about how we use electricity, and also how we waste it! We hope to do more energy saving in the future.

C
The eco-friendly project was too expensive for our home. We won't make any more changes because of the cost, and we're starting to regret that we did it at all.

D
We're glad our home is more eco-friendly now. Although it makes it more difficult to move around the house, the changes are good for the environment and that's what matters.

READING PART 5

Questions 26 – 35

Read the text below and choose the correct word for each space.
For each question, mark the correct letter **A**, **B**, **C** or **D**.

Example:

0 A that   **B** if   **C** which   **D** who

Answer: 0 | A ▆▆ | B ▭ | C ▭ | D ▭ |

Dolphins

Did you know **(0)** _____ dolphins are not fish? They are mammals just like us **(26)** _____ so are their relatives, whales. Dolphins **(27)** _____ babies, just as humans do, and the babies drink their mothers' milk. Dolphins can live for more **(28)** _____ twenty years. They also breathe air like we do, so they **(29)** _____ to come up for a breath of air. They can stay under water for up to fifteen minutes. On the other hand, fish breathe underwater and they lay eggs.

There are about 40 types of dolphin, and they are found in oceans and seas all over the world, although they **(30)** _____ shallow water. Dolphins are usually grey in colour, but they can be blue or white or even pink. They can **(31)** _____ to a length of nine and a half metres, but their **(32)** _____ size is between two and six metres. They live in groups of about twelve, but sometimes there might be as **(33)** _____ as 1,000 dolphins or even more in a single group if there is a **(34)** _____ of food in one place.

Dolphins are very intelligent animals, and they are particularly friendly towards humans. People who have been lucky enough to swim and play **(35)** _____ dolphins say that it is an experience they will never forget.

26	**A** but	**B** and	**C** like	**D** too
27	**A** do	**B** make	**C** have	**D** give
28	**A** than	**B** as	**C** from	**D** then
29	**A** must	**B** should	**C** ought	**D** need
30	**A** prefer	**B** insist	**C** demand	**D** stay
31	**A** change	**B** be	**C** live	**D** grow
32	**A** middle	**B** daily	**C** average	**D** large
33	**A** much	**B** many	**C** long	**D** big
34	**A** some	**B** few	**C** lot	**D** lots
35	**A** with	**B** at	**C** to	**D** for

WRITING PART 1

Questions 1 – 5

Here are some sentences about a girl with a cat.
For each question, complete the second sentence so that it means the same as the first.
Use no more than three words.
Write only the missing words.
You may use this page for any rough work.

Example:

0   Hazel prefers playing with her cat to watching TV.

Hazel likes playing with her cat _____ watching TV.

Answer: | **0** | *more than*

1   Hazel got her cat six months ago.

Hazel has had her cat _____ *for* _____ six months.

2   'Don't get a dog unless you've got a garden,' Hazel's teacher said.
'If you *don't have / do not have / haven't got / have not got* a garden, don't get a dog,' Hazel's teacher said.

3   Hazel thinks looking after her cat is easy.

Hazel thinks it isn't _____ *difficult/hard to* _____ look after her cat.

4   Hazel has just started buying cat food with her own money.

Hazel didn't use _____ *to buy* _____ cat food with her own money.

5   Hazel gives her cat enough food and water to keep it healthy.

Hazel's cat is _____ *given* _____ enough food and water to keep it healthy.

WRITING `PART 2`

Question 6

You want to tell your school friend about a story-writing competition.

Write a note to your friend. In your note, you should:

- tell your friend when the competition is on.
- ask your friend to take part in it.
- tell your friend when to call you to talk about this.

Write **35–45 words**.

Students' own answers

WRITING `PART 3`

Write an answer to **one** of the questions (**7** or **8**) in this part.
Write your answer in about **100 words**.

Question 7

- This is part of a letter you receive from a friend who is going on a camping trip.

> *I know you went camping last year and you said it was a great adventure. I've never done anything like this before. What can you tell me about it? What will I need to take with me for the trip?*

- Now write a **letter** to your friend.

Question 8

- Your English teacher has asked you to write a story.
- Your story must begin with this sentence:

    That morning, I wasn't expecting any visitors.

- Write your **story**.

Students' own answers

LISTENING PART 1

Questions 1 – 7

There are seven questions in this part.
For each question, choose the correct answer **A**, **B** or **C**.

Example: What job might the boy do?

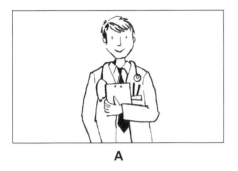

A

B

C

---

1 What did Dennis leave at school?

A

B

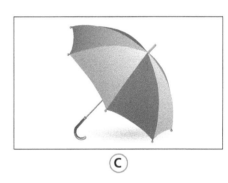

C

---

2 What is the boy having a problem with?

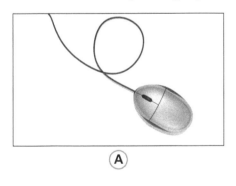

A

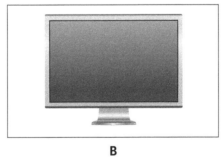

B

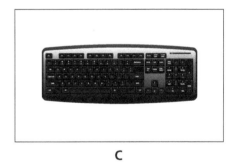

C

---

3 Where is the man going first?

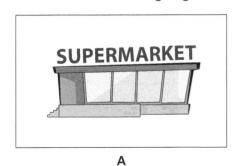

A

B

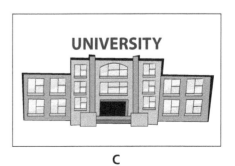

C

4 What did Irene injure the most?

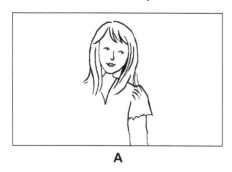

A

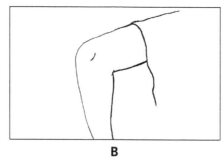

B

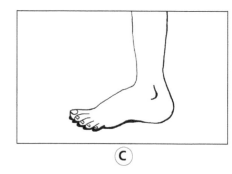

C

5 What's the last programme about?

A

B

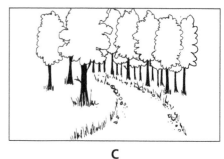

C

6 What does the girl order?

A

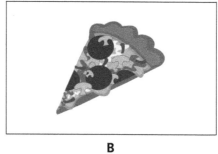

B

C

7 What sport does the girl want to do?

A

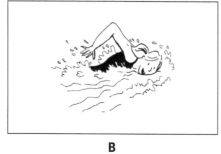

B

C

LISTENING PART 2

Questions 8 – 13

You will hear a teenager called Jack Laird talking about moving to another country.
For each question, choose the correct answer **A, B** or **C.**

8 What opportunity did Jack have before he moved?

  A to use a dictionary

  B to learn Spanish at school

  C to get a job in Spain

9 Before Jack went to live in Spain,

  A he had some experience of hot weather.

  B he used to live in a hot climate.

  C he had spent his summers in Scotland.

10 What advice does Jack give about clothes?

  A Make sure you have clothes to suit the climate.

  B Buy lots of new clothes.

  C Take as many clothes as possible.

11 When they moved, Jack's mum couldn't

  A find any sausages.

  B buy anything she wanted.

  C make the breakfast Jack likes.

12 How did Jack feel at first?

  A He was enjoying himself.

  B He was lonely and shy.

  C It was easy to meet other teenagers.

13 Jack thinks moving to another country

  A is sure to be a great adventure.

  B is a good way to make friends.

  C is easier if you prepare well.

LISTENING PART 3

Questions 14 – 19

You will hear some public announcements at an airport.
For each question, fill in the missing information in the numbered space.

AIRPORT ANNOUNCEMENTS

Delay

Edinburgh flight delay: **(14)** _____*three/3*_____ hours

Services

Change money: Terminal **(15)** _____*A*_____

For help, ask at: the **(16)** _____*information*_____ desk in Terminal A

Airport security

Security staff might ask for: your **(17)** _____*boarding pass*_____

Security staff will remove: **(18)** _____*luggage/bags*_____ left alone

Important message

John MacDonald to go to: **(19)** _____*passport control*_____

LISTENING PART 4

Questions 20 – 25

Look at the six sentences for this part.
You will hear a conversation between a girl, Jill, and a boy, Nick, about food.
Decide if each sentence is correct or incorrect.
If it is correct, choose the letter **A** for **YES**. If it is not correct, choose the letter **B** for **NO**.

		YES	NO
20	Nick wants to eat in a restaurant.	A	(B)
21	They both want to have a pizza.	A	(B)
22	Nick has made food for Jill before.	A	(B)
23	Jill has never made an omelette before.	(A)	B
24	Milk is an essential ingredient in an omelette.	A	(B)
25	Jill would rather eat fruit than ice cream.	(A)	B

SPEAKING PART 1

2–3 minutes (3–4 minutes for a group of three)

Phase 1

This part is always the same. See page 30 of Test 1.

Phase 2
Interlocutor *(Select one or more questions from the list to ask each candidate. Use candidates' names throughout. Ask Candidate B first.)*

What hobbies do you enjoy doing in your free time? Why?
What is your favourite sport? Why?
Who is your favourite sportsperson? Why?
What sport do you enjoy watching on TV? Why?
What new sport or hobby would you like to learn to do? Why?
Thank you.

Introduction to Part 2
In the next part, you are going to talk to each other.

Students' own answers

SPEAKING PART 2

2–3 minutes (3 minutes for a group of three)

Learning English

Interlocutor
(Say to both candidates)

I'm going to describe a situation to you.
A friend of yours is interested in **learning English** and he would like some **advice** on **the best way to learn**. Talk together about the **different ways** of learning English and then decide which would be **the best**.

See pictures on page 177

Here is a picture with some ideas to help you.

I'll say that again.
A friend of yours is interested in **learning English** and he would like some **advice** on **the best way to learn**. Talk together about the **different ways** of learning English and then decide which would be **the best**.
All right? Talk together.

(Allow the candidates enough time to complete the task without intervention. Prompt only if necessary.)

Thank you.

Students' own answers

SPEAKING PART 3

At the doctor's

3 minutes (4 minutes for a group of three)

Interlocutor *(Say to both candidates)*	Now, I'd like each of you to talk on your own about something. I'm going to give each of you a photograph of people **at the doctor's**.

See photo A on page 178

(Candidate A), here is your photograph. Please show it to (Candidate B), but I'd like you to talk about it. (Candidate B), you just listen. I'll give you your photograph in a moment. (Candidate A), please tell us what you can see in your photograph.

Candidate A *(Approximately 1 minute)*
(If there is a need to intervene, prompts rather than direct questions should be used.)

Interlocutor Thank you.

See photo B on page 178

Now, (Candidate B), here is your photograph. It also shows **people at the doctor's**. Please show it to (Candidate A) and tell us what you can see in the photograph.

Candidate B *(Approximately 1 minute)*
(If there is a need to intervene, prompts rather than direct questions should be used.)

Interlocutor Thank you.

SPEAKING PART 4

3 minutes (3–4 minutes for a group of three)

Interlocutor *(Say to both candidates)*	Your photographs showed people **at the doctor's**. Now, I'd like you to talk together about the times **you** have been **to the doctor's** and **how you felt** about it.

(Allow the candidates enough time to complete the task without intervention. Prompt only if necessary.)

Thank you. That's the end of the test.

Students' own answers

READING PART 1

Questions 1 – 5

Look at the text in each question.
What does it say?
Mark the correct letter **A**, **B** or **C**.

Example:

0

> **FREE TO A GOOD HOME:**
> two black and white puppies.
> Jack and Jill, 3 months old.
> Need lots of exercise and space to play.
> Would suit a family.
> Phone Tina: 0842 143 974

The advert says the puppies

A have already got names.

B are playful and fun.

C are from the same family.

Answer: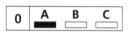

1

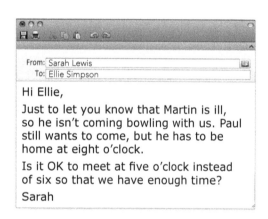

From: Sarah Lewis
To: Ellie Simpson

Hi Ellie,

Just to let you know that Martin is ill, so he isn't coming bowling with us. Paul still wants to come, but he has to be home at eight o'clock.

Is it OK to meet at five o'clock instead of six so that we have enough time?

Sarah

Sarah wants to know

A if Ellie can meet up earlier than planned.

B if Paul wants to go bowling with them.

C if eight o'clock is too late to get home.

2

3.30 PM

Mum,

Drama class isn't on today because Mrs Hooper is ill, so I'm coming straight home from school. See you soon.

Lily

What does Lily say?

A She doesn't feel well.

B Her class is cancelled.

C Her teacher sent her home.

3

The school library is a place where students can read or do homework. It is NOT the playground so please don't talk loudly or run around. Food and drink are not allowed.

The sign says the library is a place where

A   students should be quiet.

B   students can eat lunch in peace.

C   students can get help with homework.

4

Tim Carlton says...

Can I borrow your black jacket for the party on Saturday, please? My brother said I could borrow his jacket, but it's brown and doesn't suit me. Bring it to school on Friday, if that's OK.

A   Tim prefers his brother's clothes to his own.

B   Tim is going to a party on Friday night.

C   Tim doesn't have a suitable jacket for the party.

5

BOAT RACE!

Saturday from 3 pm at Green Park Lake.

All teams should sign up before Thursday to take part.

Big prizes for the winners!

What should teams do?

A   Arrive at the lake on time.

B   Register before the race.

C   Meet at the park on Thursday.

READING PART 2

Questions 6 – 10

The teenagers below are all looking for a new penfriend.
On the opposite page, there are descriptions of eight people who also want to find penfriends.
Decide which person would be the most suitable for the following teenagers.
For questions **6 – 10**, mark the correct letter (**A – H**).

6

Mark is British and he wants to write to someone from a different country. He would like to learn a new language and learn about a different culture.

F

7

Ruth is interested in outdoor activities. She would like to have a penfriend that she could write to about travelling and get some advice on nice places to visit.

C

8

Luke wants a penfriend who is the same age as him. He is interested in computer games and new technology and would like a penfriend with the same interests.

H

9

Alicia would like to write to someone who loves animals as much as she does. She also wants a penfriend who is older and can give her advice.

E

10

Adrian would like a penfriend that he could go and visit. He likes reading and photography, and would like to write to someone about his hobbies.

D

Penfriends

A Hello, I'm Carol and I just love books! I would like to be a famous writer one day with my books in the bookshops and my photo in all the newspapers! I also like doing sports; my favourite is cycling. When I'm at home, I spend most of my time on my computer, writing messages to friends or downloading music.

B Hello. I'm Lucy and I live in France. I've only been living here for a month, though, and can't really speak any French yet. I'm still learning about the culture here too. It's very different to life in the UK. I miss lots of things from back home, so would like to write to someone from there. Maybe we could even visit each other!

C I'm Sonja and I love camping, hiking and spending time outside. I'm pretty sporty too! I would love to move to India one day. I went there with my family last year and loved it! Indian culture is just amazing! I always go to interesting places with my family and we normally go on holiday twice a year. When I'm old enough, I definitely want to see more of the world!

D I'm Olivia and I live in the countryside. My friends always laugh at me because I don't go anywhere without my camera. You just never know when you're going to see something amazing! My house is always busy because I always have friends to stay. When I'm not out and about, you'll find me in my dad's library – my favourite room in the house!

E Hello. I'm Gail and I'm sixteen. I live on a farm with my family and I help out with the farm work. I milk the cows, feed the chickens and look after the horses. I really enjoy spending time with the animals, even if it does mean I get very dirty! I am the oldest of four girls so my sisters always come to me if they have a problem or need help with something.

F Hi. My name's Hans and I'm from Germany. I like visiting new places around Germany and making new friends from all over the world! I can speak German, English and Spanish. I really want to visit the UK and would like to find out what life is like, what food people eat and how people celebrate there.

G Hi. I'm Henry and I've got a big family – if you count all the pets, that is! We have three cats, two dogs and four budgies. My parents work for an animal charity and really care about animals. I'm not so sure though. Of course I like them, but the house is normally so noisy that it drives me crazy! When I'm older, I'll have one dog and that's it!

H My name's Ben, and I'm fourteen. I spend a lot of time inside playing on my laptop and I love finding new, interesting websites. My favourite things are my MP3 player and my smartphone; I don't think I could live without them! I enjoy writing emails, and it would be fun to have a penfriend who is just like me!

READING PART 3

Questions 11 – 20

Look at the sentences below about about a science fair.
Read the text on the opposite page to decide if each sentence is correct or incorrect.
If it is correct, mark **A**.
If it is not correct, mark **B**.

11	Students had one day to create and present a science project.	A	**(B)**
12	There was a variety of projects that involved different science-related topics.	**(A)**	B
13	The winning project used a complicated scientific method to create power.	A	**(B)**
14	Someone from the winning team said that making the train had been enjoyable.	**(A)**	B
15	Everyone believed that the most important thing was to be the winner.	A	**(B)**
16	Mr Keel said that students learn more than just science by taking part in the fair.	**(A)**	B
17	Ms Gray disagreed with the science teacher's opinion.	A	**(B)**
18	According to Ms Gray, students enjoy reading about science experiments.	A	**(B)**
19	The school provides practical experiences over a range of subjects.	**(A)**	B
20	There will be other science fairs at the school over the next two weeks.	A	**(B)**

Lakeside School Science Fair

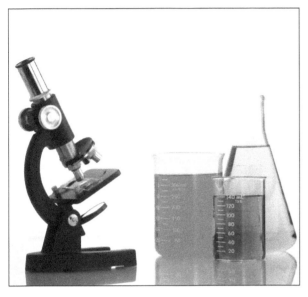

'This year's school science fair was a complete success,' says Lakeside School head teacher, Ms Gray. 'All the students worked really hard on their science projects, and the results were brilliant!'

School students at Lakeside School spent weeks thinking up, planning and making science projects for the one-day science fair yesterday. The school hall was packed with enthusiastic students and impressed teachers as the students showed off their projects. One group of students made a working volcano, while another group built a small wind farm using small pieces of wood and cardboard. There was a wide range of models which were the result of students' experiments on topics like energy, nature and physics. Students of all ages took part and worked hard to get ready for the big day.

Science teachers picked the top three projects and presented awards to the groups. The top prize this year went to a group of year-ten students who made a working steam train. They used a heating system to turn water into steam and used that steam to power the train. Simple, but effective! 'We are so glad that they liked our project,' Ken from the steam-train team said. 'We worked really hard on it, but it was also really good fun!' Most of the students agree that it was more about the experience than who won. 'It's just really fun to work on a science project and build something yourself,' said Emma, 13.

Teachers also think that the yearly school fair is about much more than just prizes. Science teacher Ed Keel says, 'Fairs like this one really help students to work as part of a team. They find answers to problems together and feel proud of making something or achieving something themselves. That's really the most important thing.' A similar message was given by the head teacher, who considers events like this to be a big step in young people's education. 'Students prefer to do something practical and to experiment with science, rather than just reading about it or copying from text books. That's why the school runs events like the science fair,' she said. The school believes that these kinds of experiences are necessary for learning. That is why the teaching staff also organise new unusual sports activities, arts and crafts workshops and a drama group which acts out plays about historic events.

The exhibition of the projects will remain in the school hall for the next two weeks so that parents and people from the local community can come and see what the students have created. All in all, the event was a huge success. Students were happy to get involved and everyone enjoyed the day.

READING PART 4

Questions 21 – 25

Read the text and questions below.
For each question, mark the correct letter **A**, **B**, **C** or **D**.

The World of Facebook

Sixteen-year-old Darren tells us about the popular social networking website, Facebook, and what he thinks about it.

For me, Facebook is about staying in touch with friends, whether that means writing on someone's 'wall' or sending them a private message. It's a useful website for finding long-lost friends, arranging parties and sharing photos. But that's not all: Facebook is now being used by all kinds of people for all kinds of reasons!

Do you want to play computer games? Log on to Facebook. There are now thousands of entertaining games and puzzles to help you pass the time. Do you want to find cafés, cinemas and bowling alleys in your area? Log on to Facebook. Thousands of businesses are now advertising, and they have Facebook pages that you can join and 'like', which makes it very easy to search for fun things to do near you. I think it's brilliant to have all the information that you want on just one website!

People are now joining Facebook to make professional connections too, either with people who do the same kind of work, or with businesses that are looking for new people to work for them.

It's a pretty good idea since so many people use Facebook these days, especially young people! Even students log on to Facebook to look for summer or part-time jobs.

And that's not all! Now there are hundreds of pages about sports teams, TV programmes and pop stars to look at on Facebook. However, I believe the main reason most young people use Facebook is because it's so easy to let the world know what you think about different things or people, whether it's about a new film at the cinema, or whether you prefer Rihanna with long or short hair. You can even write comments directly on other people's Facebook pages including some stars' pages. But you have to be careful because giving your opinion online can be dangerous.

We mustn't forget that Facebook is meant to be fun and shouldn't be used for saying bad things about people around us. I recently read a news article about a student who had to leave school because she made rude and unfair comments about a teacher on her Facebook wall. Several other school students have been in trouble for similar comments and opinions. In fact, it really annoys me when I see somebody has written nasty things about another person!

It's true that Facebook is becoming more and more part of our daily lives for many different reasons, and it can be really helpful as well as being a lot of fun. But, as with all websites, we must be careful about how we use it.

21 What is Darren doing in the text?

    A Warning about how dangerous websites are.

    B Giving his opinion on one website and saying how it is used.

    C Giving advice about how to spend your time.

    D Persuading the reader not to use websites like this one.

22 What does Darren say about Facebook?

    A It is useful for finding information about local entertainment.

    B It is confusing because it has too many uses.

    C It is mainly used for social reasons these days.

    D It is useless for people advertising their businesses.

23 Why does Darren think young people like Facebook so much?

    A It's the best place to find information about sport.

    B It's a good place to read film reviews.

    C They like having the opportunity to give their opinions.

    D They can have conversations about their interests.

24 According to Darren, what should people avoid doing on Facebook?

    A giving opinions about teachers

    B writing anything about other people

    C making comments that might hurt people

    D enjoying themselves

25 What might Darren say to sum up his article?

A
> Facebook is a good resource, but it encourages young people and students to behave badly.

B
> Facebook is used more by businesses these days, but schools often check to see what their students are writing.

C
> Facebook is used for many different reasons, but you should still always take care when using websites like this.

D
> Facebook is useful and fun, but now it is only used by people looking for jobs and people who want to play games.

Practice Test 6

READING PART 5

Questions 26 – 35

Read the text below and choose the correct word for each space.
For each question, mark the correct letter **A**, **B**, **C** or **D**.

Example:

0 **A** over   **B** in   **C** under   **D** on

Answer: 0   [A █ B ☐ C ☐ D ☐]

Sport

Sport is a big part of daily life for people all **(0)** _____ the world. It is a great way to get both exercise and entertainment, **(26)** _____ you are playing as part of a team in games **(27)** _____ as football or rugby, or playing against a friend, for example in golf or bowling.

Many people believe that a lot of sports first **(28)** _____ in Ancient Greece, especially since Greeks invented the Olympic Games almost 2,800 years ago. However, we now know that the Chinese and Egyptians were taking part in sport long before **(29)** _____. Gymnastics, swimming and fishing were **(30)** _____ the sports popular in Egypt as early **(31)** _____ 2000 BC.

These days, we enjoy traditional sports like running and horse-riding as **(32)** _____ as more modern games, and there is an endless choice when it comes to exercising and taking part in sports. Some of the more modern sports are handball, motocross and, **(33)** _____ course, extreme sports like kitesurfing.

Sports play an important role in our lives right from childhood, **(34)** _____ are an excellent way to **(35)** _____ fit and healthy.

26	**A** whether	**B** unless	**C** either	**D** though
27	**A** so	**B** such	**C** similar	**D** same
28	**A** entered	**B** showed	**C** appeared	**D** came
29	**A** then	**B** there	**C** these	**D** those
30	**A** between	**B** among	**C** inside	**D** beside
31	**A** for	**B** since	**C** to	**D** as
32	**A** well	**B** far	**C** long	**D** easy
33	**A** in	**B** with	**C** off	**D** of
34	**A** also	**B** addition	**C** and	**D** too
35	**A** have	**B** hold	**C** keep	**D** stand

WRITING PART 1

Questions 1 – 5

Here are some sentences about two best friends.
For each question, complete the second sentence so that it means the same as the first.
Use no more than three words.
Write only the missing words.
You may use this page for any rough work.

Example:

0   Sam and Paul have known each other for six years.

Sam and Paul first _____ six years ago.

Answer: | **0** | *met* |

---

1   Sam goes to a different school from Paul.

Paul and Sam _____ *do not / don't go* _____ to the same school.

2   Paul is happy to play games with Sam's school friends.

Paul enjoys _____ *playing* _____ games with Sam's school friends.

3   The boys joined the same football team last year.

The boys have _____ *been / played / been playing* in the same football team for one year.

4   Paul was allowed to stay at Sam's house at the weekend.

Paul's mum _____ *let* _____ him stay at Sam's house at the weekend.

5   'Do you want to go camping with me and my parents?' Paul asked Sam.

Paul asked Sam _____ *if/whether he wanted* _____ to go camping with him and his parents.

WRITING PART 2

Question 6

You arranged to meet your friend yesterday at the shopping centre, but you forgot about it.

Write an email to your friend to apologise. In your email, you should:

- tell your friend that you're sorry
- explain what happened
- suggest another time when you can meet.

Write **35–45 words**.

Students' own answers

WRITING PART 3

Write an answer to **one** of the questions (**7** or **8**) in this part.
Write your answer in about **100 words**.

Question 7

- This is part of a letter you receive from an English friend.

> *A famous person has offered to give money to our school. What equipment do you think our school needs? How will this help the students?*

- Now write a **letter** to your friend.

Question 8

- Your teacher has asked you to write a story for homework.
- Your story must begin with this sentence:

    It was a dark and rainy night, but Sally wasn't scared.

- Write your **story**.

Students' own answers

LISTENING PART 1

Questions 1 – 7

There are seven questions in this part.
For each question, choose the correct answer **A**, **B** or **C**.

Example: What is the boy's favourite thing in his bedroom?

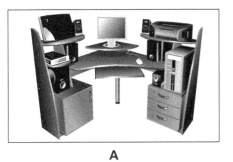

A

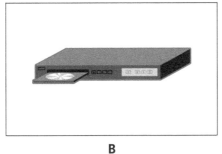

B

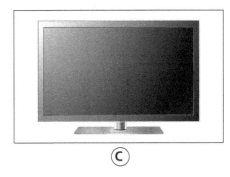

Ⓒ

1 Where will Tony meet his friend?

Ⓐ

B

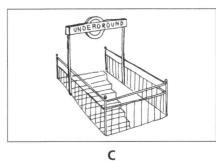

C

2 How will Gail get into town?

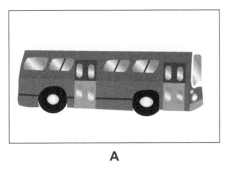

A

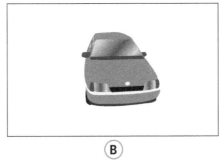

Ⓑ

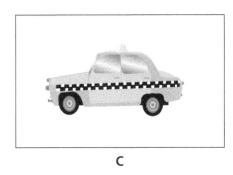

C

3 What will be on the radio tonight?

A

Ⓑ

C

4 What is David going to do?

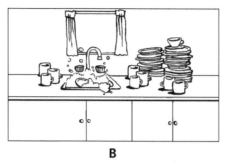

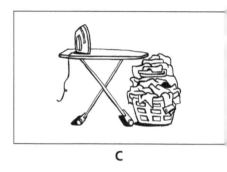

A | B | C

5 Which is the first sports day event?

A | B | C

6 What is Hannah going to do at the weekend?

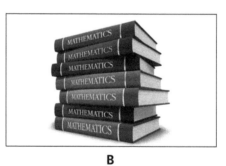

A | B | C

7 Which animal does Tony's family have?

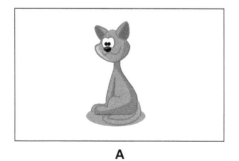

A | B | C

LISTENING PART 2

Questions 8 – 13

You will hear part of an interview with a boy called Matt Morris who is talking about school rules and how he feels about them. For each question, choose the correct answer **A**, **B** or **C**.

8   What does Matt think about school rules?

   A They are necessary.

   B He doesn't know the reason for them.

   C There shouldn't be so many.

9   The school that Matt goes to

   A has lots of students.

   B has very strict rules.

   C has large classes but no dining room.

10   Detention in school

   A isn't as important as homework.

   B happens on weekdays and weekends.

   C is always given to people who break the rules.

11   Matt thinks that

   A students who behave badly should spend extra time at school.

   B most teachers don't understand students.

   C making difficult students stay behind after school is a bad idea.

12   How does Matt feel about school uniforms?

   A They aren't very fashionable.

   B They have good and bad points.

   C They make people anxious about how they look.

13   How would Matt change the school day?

   A He would make it shorter.

   B He would have outdoor classes.

   C He would have more breaks during the day.

LISTENING PART 3

Questions 14 – 19

You will hear a recipe for a dessert.
For each question, fill in the missing information in the numbered space.

Recipe of the Week

Recipe for: **(14)** _____chocolate cake_____

PREPARATION:

Oven temperature: **(15)** _____180_____ degrees

INGREDIENTS

175g of butter

165g of **(16)** _____sugar_____

150g of **(17)** _____flour_____

50g of cocoa

Three large eggs

One teaspoon of baking powder

COOKING:

Baking time: **(18)** _____forty-five/45_____ minutes

Cake ready: when **(19)** _____fork_____ is clean

LISTENING PART 4

Questions 20 – 25

Look at the six sentences for this part.
You will hear a conversation between a girl, Nancy, and a boy, Dan, about a friend who has a broken leg.
Decide if each sentence is correct or incorrect.
If it is correct, choose the letter **A** for **YES**. If it is not correct, choose the letter **B** for **NO**.

		YES	NO
20	Dan thinks having a broken leg means you can't do sport.	(A)	B
21	Nancy says having a broken leg makes everyday tasks more challenging.	(A)	B
22	Dan says he likes being independent.	(A)	B
23	Dan thinks having a broken arm is worse than having a broken leg.	A	(B)
24	Nancy thinks having a broken leg is worse than having a broken arm.	A	(B)
25	Nancy believes Vicky is unhappy about staying at home.	(A)	B

SPEAKING PART 1

2–3 minutes (3–4 minutes for a group of three)

Phase 1

This part is always the same. See page 30 of Test 1.

Phase 2

Interlocutor *(Select one or more questions from the list to ask each candidate. Use candidates' names throughout. Ask Candidate B first.)*

Where do you usually go on holiday? What do you do there?
What time of year do you most enjoy going on holiday? Why?
Where would you most like to go on holiday?
What was the worst holiday you've been on? Why?
Who do you like to go on holiday with? Why?
Thank you.

Introduction to Part 2
In the next part, you are going to talk to each other.

Students' own answers

SPEAKING PART 2

2–3 minutes (3 minutes for a group of three)

Winter Holidays

Interlocutor
(Say to both candidates)

I'm going to describe a situation to you.
You are **going on a winter holiday** in France. It is **very cold** and you will be staying at a **hotel** high up in the mountains. Talk together about the **different things** you could take on a winter holiday and then decide which are the **most important**.
Here is a picture with some ideas to help you.

See pictures on page 179

I'll say that again.
You are **going on a winter holiday** in France. It is **very cold** and you will be staying at a **hotel** high up in the mountains. Talk together about the **different things** you could take on a winter holiday and then decide which are the **most important**.
All right? Talk together.

(Allow the candidates enough time to complete the task without intervention. Prompt only if necessary.)

Thank you.

Students' own answers

SPEAKING PART 3

3 minutes (4 minutes for a group of three)

Doing housework

Interlocutor *(Say to both candidates)*	Now, I'd like each of you to talk on your own about something. I'm going to give each of you a photograph of someone **doing housework**.
See photo A on page 180	*(Candidate A)*, here is your photograph. Please show it to *(Candidate B)*, but I'd like you to talk about it. *(Candidate B)*, you just listen. I'll give you your photograph in a moment. *(Candidate A)*, please tell us what you can see in your photograph.

Candidate A *(Approximately 1 minute)*
(If there is a need to intervene, prompts rather than direct questions should be used.)

Interlocutor See photo B on page 180	Thank you. Now, *(Candidate B)*, here is your photograph. It also shows someone **doing housework**. Please show it to *(Candidate A)* and tell us what you can see in the photograph.

Candidate B *(Approximately 1 minute)*
(If there is a need to intervene, prompts rather than direct questions should be used.)

Interlocutor	Thank you.

SPEAKING PART 4

3 minutes (3–4 minutes for a group of three)

Interlocutor *(Say to both candidates)*	Your photographs showed people **doing housework**. Now, I'd like you to talk together about the **the kind of housework you do** and **why** you think **housework is important**.

(Allow the candidates enough time to complete the task without intervention. Prompt only if necessary.)

Thank you. That's the end of the test.

Students' own answers

Practice Test 7

READING PART 1

Questions 1 – 5

Look at the text in each question.
What does it say?
Mark the correct letter **A**, **B** or **C**.

Example:

0

> Nina,
> I'll be late. Lunch is in the oven for you and Simon. Heat it for five minutes. Call me if there's any problem.
> Mum
> PS If Mr Dickinson calls, get his number and I'll call him back.

The note says that

A Nina's mum will phone Mr Dickinson back if he calls.

B Nina's mum hasn't cooked lunch yet.

C Nina and Simon must remember to call her.

Answer:

1

> 12:20 PM
> Daniel,
> Meeting Josh at the park to go for a jog. If you want to join us, call me and I'll explain where we are.
> Brian

How can Daniel find where to meet his friends?

A He can go for a jog.

B He can meet them at the park.

C He can phone Brian.

2

> **FOR SALE**
> Almost new smartphone still in its box
> Lots of games and other applications on already
> Call 937764410 for info

The advertisement says that

A you can do many things with this phone.

B the phone is new.

C someone wants to buy a smartphone.

3

No entrance to the lab without permission

If you need to use it, contact Ms Green in the teachers' room during school hours.

Who can use the lab?

A   only Ms Green

B   nobody during school hours

C   students with permission

4

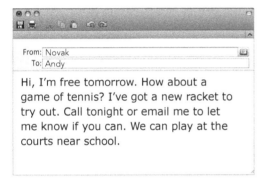

From: Novak
To: Andy

Hi, I'm free tomorrow. How about a game of tennis? I've got a new racket to try out. Call tonight or email me to let me know if you can. We can play at the courts near school.

Why has Novak written this email?

A   to tell Andy about his new racket

B   to invite Andy to play tennis

C   to inform Andy about the tennis courts

5

SWEATER LOST

Green with blue stripes. It wasn't expensive, but I love it! Left it at school today. If you find it, please call Jeff on 2345567890. Thanks.

Why does Jeff want his sweater back?

A   He really likes it.

B   It's a cheap sweater.

C   It's a school sweater.

READING PART 2

Questions 6 – 10

The teenagers below are all looking for a place to have a celebration.
On the opposite page, there are descriptions of eight places where people can go to celebrate.
Decide which place would be the most suitable for the following teenagers.
For questions **6 – 10**, mark the correct letter (**A – H**).

---

6  Danny is looking for a place to eat out with his three best friends to celebrate his birthday. He would like an inexpensive Italian restaurant, which has rock music, for an early evening meal.

H

7  Samantha would like to find a place to dance to pop music with her classmates to celebrate the end of the school year. It should be easy to get to and it should also serve snacks and drinks.

F

8  Tamara wants to find a place to arrange a surprise anniversary celebration for her parents on Monday. The venue must have a romantic atmosphere and it should serve good food to remind them of their holiday in France.

C

9  Costas would like to find a place to invite his friends to celebrate winning a tennis tournament. He's looking for cheap tasty food near some sports facilities where they can do some sport before they eat.

E

10 Tina and two friends want to give their friend, Marina, a surprise dinner as a birthday present. They want a place in a central location that is suitable for vegetarians and that serves Indian or Chinese food, or both.

A

Restaurant and club guide

A   **Bombay Palace** is an exotic restaurant which serves delicious Indian and Chinese food. It is open every day of the week and you can book a table for four at a special price. There is an amazing variety of dishes, including vegetarian, for all tastes and budgets. It is conveniently located in the city centre.

B   **Mama Italia** is opening this week. Delicious food, made by a famous Italian chef, a great atmosphere with classical music and opera in the background and luxurious decor. The waiting list is very long, so if you want to experience eating at this restaurant, you must reserve a table at least two weeks ahead.

C   **Le Bon Temps** is one of the most amazing restaurants in town. It serves excellent French food in a friendly and relaxed atmosphere and at reasonable prices. Suitable for a romantic dinner for two on special occasions. It also has its own car park. Open all week.

D   **Agora** is the club of the year. Great, energetic atmosphere, friendly waiters, fantastic hip-hop music and live bands – open all night every night. On the outskirts of the city, away from busy areas. You need a car to get there, but it's worth the effort! Every weekend, special guest DJs! Over eighteens only.

E   **Chester's Café** is the ideal place for those who want to enjoy themselves with some energetic activity. Open all day, the café offers a variety of healthy refreshments and snacks. Our customers can take the opportunity to use the facilities to play table tennis or bowling at prices that everyone can afford.

F   **The Stars** is the new club in town. Fantastic modern music, rock, pop, hip-hop and rap, with great DJs every evening. Located in the city centre, you can dance and have fun all night long. Small snacks and soft drinks make the club suitable for people under eighteen. If the weather is good, you can enjoy our outdoor area. Book early for large groups.

G   **Eden** is a vegetarian restaurant which serves traditional Italian and Greek dishes. The food is fresh and well-cooked and it's in a place that's easy for everyone in the town to reach. It's open from Tuesday to Saturday. We apologise for being closed on Mondays.

H   **Mario's Diner** is a great surprise for those who visit it. The Italian food is home-made and tasty, the atmosphere is friendly and fun, the rock music is up-to-date, and it's open from late afternoon until late in the evening every day of the week. Visit it if you enjoy delicious food made with the freshest of ingredients, at prices which are affordable.

READING PART 3

Questions 11 – 20

Look at the sentences below about a sports centre.
Read the text on the opposite page to decide if each sentence is correct or incorrect.
If it is correct, mark **A**.
If it is not correct, mark **B**.

11	Sunshine Sports Centre is in the city centre.	A	(B)
12	There is a special swimming pool for younger children.	(A)	B
13	Members can come and play football at any time without booking.	A	(B)
14	The sports centre's personal trainers can put you on a special diet.	A	(B)
15	You can have lessons alone or in a group.	(A)	B
16	There are special programmes for younger people at the sports centre.	(A)	B
17	The lifeguard is on duty when the swimming pool is open.	(A)	B
18	You can take food from the restaurant and have a picnic in the garden.	A	(B)
19	You can do sport at the centre to celebrate your birthday.	(A)	B
20	If you want to have a party, you must bring your own music.	A	(B)

Sunshine Sports Centre

One of the most modern sports centres in town, the Sunshine Sports Centre is not just a sports club but much more! Just a few kilometres from the centre of town in a clean, green neighbourhood next to a park, Sunshine Sports Centre offers entertainment for the whole family.

Facilities

With a swimming pool for adults and teens, and a smaller one for children, our centre has something for all the members of the family. Parents can relax while children play in the water. For anybody who is interested in competitive sports, our volleyball, tennis and basketball courts are the ideal place to work off stress. Our centre also has two five-a-side football pitches. You can reserve the pitches to play with your teammates, but book early – they're very popular!

Whether you just want to keep in shape, lose some weight or build your strength, there's the gym with its super-modern equipment and three personal trainers to look after you and answer all your questions. They can also give you general advice about healthy eating and dieting.

Lessons

It doesn't matter if you're five or eighty-five, there's something for you at the Sunshine Sports Centre! We offer personal training in all sports if you want it, but there are also group lessons for all sports if you prefer teamwork.

Kids and teenagers

Take advantage of our special offer for younger members. For members between five and sixteen years old, there are special lessons in water polo, competitive swimming and diving. There are many classes for all levels of swimmers, with a lifeguard on duty from nine in the morning when the pool opens until it closes at seven in the evening.

Social events

Sunshine Sports Centre is not only for sport! You can enjoy a delicious meal prepared with fresh, organic ingredients at our restaurant or have a milkshake with your friends on the balcony overlooking the swimming pool and the courts. In addition, there are lovely gardens where families or friends can have a picnic when the weather is good. When it isn't, you can come indoors and play table tennis, darts or go bowling! To celebrate a birthday, there is no better place than the Sunshine Sports Centre. It is the ideal venue for a party, especially for teenagers. As well as listening to great music from our resident DJ, you can make use of the sports facilities and the restaurant.

So, come on! Sign up for Sunshine Sports Centre today!

READING PART 4

Questions 21 – 25

Read the text and questions below.
For each question, mark the correct letter **A**, **B**, **C** or **D**.

How to raise money for charity

Fifteen year old Michael Branson gives some tips to those interested in supporting a charity.

Looking for an original way to raise money for charity? Has your school run out of clever and fun ideas? Don't give up! There are several ways to support your favourite charity and enjoy yourselves at the same time.

How about holding a bean bath competition? 'How does this help?' you may ask yourselves. Well, it's very simple really – you agree to sit in a bath full of baked beans, then for every minute you stay in it, people pay money! The longer you stay in the bath, the more money you collect for the charity your school has chosen! It's extremely messy, but it's good fun! Just a piece of advice, though. Make sure you let your parents know what you're doing. Wear old clothes because they're going to need washing afterwards!

Here's another idea that we used at my school: organise a car wash. Everybody who has a car sooner or later washes it or has it washed. So why don't you and your classmates do the job? The money the car owners pay for having their cars washed will go towards your charity. When we did it, we had an amazing time! At first, some of us were worried about getting wet or dirty and it's true, we did. But we also had fun, and at the end of the day it was really worth it!

On the other hand, if you don't feel like getting wet or messy, but have some musical talent, how about organising a street concert? Street musicians can make a lot of money and so can you if you've got the talent and courage it takes to play in front of an audience. You just need to find a suitable place (make sure you're allowed to play music in that public place), practise for a few hours with your friends first, and give it a try!

I hope all these ideas have helped you a bit and, if you've got any other great suggestions, we would love to hear them. We can publish them so other people can use them, too. Good luck!

21 What is Michael doing in the text?

  A Informing readers about charity events they can go to.

  B Suggesting fun ideas for people to raise money for charity.

  C Giving advice on how to become rich.

  D Warning readers against doing some things for charity.

22 What does Michael say about bean baths?

  A You must hold as many beans as you can in your hands.

  B You can ask people to pay for you to sit in a bath full of beans.

  C You must put on old clothes after the bath.

  D You must ask your mum for permission to wash dirty clothes.

23 What is Michael's attitude towards the car wash he organised?

  A He believes it was a success.

  B He was upset about getting wet.

  C He thought some students were too worried.

  D He believes that there are better ways to collect money.

24 What does Michael say you need talent for?

  A to enjoy good music

  B to go to a concert

  C to practise before a concert

  D to play music in the street

25 What might Michael write to a friend about raising money for charity?

A You may need to ask a lot of people for permission if you want to raise money.

B Raising money for a good cause can be fun, but be prepared to get dirty.

C You need to work very hard to raise money, and it's a dirty job.

D Older people may not allow you to raise money.

READING PART 5

Questions 26 – 35

Read the text below and choose the correct word for each space.
For each question, mark the correct letter **A**, **B**, **C** or **D**.

Example:

0 A at   **B** by   **C** in   **D** to

Answer:

0	A	B	C	D
	☐	☐	▬	☐

Marie Curie

Most people have heard of Marie Curie because of her scientific discoveries, but not many people know about her background. Some people think she was born in France, but she was actually born in Poland, **(0)** _____ 1867. Her name was Marie Sklodowska and she was the youngest of five brothers and sisters. **(26)** _____ her father and grandfather were teachers, and her mother ran a boarding school for girls.

Marie's **(27)** _____ life was very difficult. Her mother and one of her sisters died when she was **(28)** _____ young, and the family lost their money, so it was very difficult for Marie to continue her studies. **(29)** _____, she managed to go to France, where she studied physics, chemistry and mathematics at Sorbonne University. As she was extremely poor, she also had to work **(30)** _____ she was studying.

A few years later in 1893, she **(31)** _____ her future husband, Pierre Curie. He was also a scientist, **(32)** _____ the same type of research. Their common interests brought **(33)** _____ together and they got married soon afterwards.

Marie, her husband Pierre Curie and Henri Becquerel won the Nobel Prize in Physics in 1903. Then Marie Curie got the Nobel Prize in Chemistry in 1911. She was the first woman to get any Nobel Prize, and the first person **(34)** _____ had ever won two Nobel Prizes. She died in 1934 and she was buried **(35)** _____ to her husband.

26	**A** And	**B** Both	**C** Either	**D** Neither
27	**A** early	**B** first	**C** late	**D** last
28	**A** before	**B** already	**C** yet	**D** still
29	**A** Though	**B** However	**C** Although	**D** Despite
30	**A** while	**B** till	**C** then	**D** from
31	**A** looked	**B** saw	**C** met	**D** knew
32	**A** taking	**B** doing	**C** making	**D** having
33	**A** them	**B** their	**C** these	**D** her
34	**A** which	**B** she	**C** what	**D** who
35	**A** beside	**B** behind	**C** next	**D** opposite

WRITING PART 1

Questions 1 – 5

Here are some sentences about a boy and his bike.
For each question, complete the second sentence so that it means the same as the first.
Use no more than three words.
Write only the missing words.
You may use this page for any rough work.

Example:

0   Kevin's mum asked him to clean his bike.

   'Please _____,' Kevin's mum said to him.

Answer: | 0 | *clean your bike* |

---

1   Kevin had his bike fixed by a man at the shop.

   A man at the shop _____*fixed Kevin's/his*_____ bike for him.

2   Kevin doesn't ride his bike when the weather is bad.

   Kevin only _____*rides*_____ his bike if the weather is good.

3   Last year Kevin wasn't old enough to ride his bike to school.

   Last year Kevin was _____*too*_____ young to ride his bike to school.

4   Kevin's bike was more expensive than mine.

   My bike wasn't _____*as expensive*_____ as Kevin's.

5   Kevin's mum thinks he should take better care of his bike.

   Kevin's mum thinks he _____*ought*_____ to take better care of his bike.

WRITING PART 2

Question 6

Your best friend, Alex, has been ill for a few days.

Write a message in a 'get well' card to Alex. In your message, you should:

- tell Alex you hope he's feeling better
- give Alex the school news
- promise to visit Alex soon.

Write **35–45 words**.

Students' own answers

WRITING PART 3

Write an answer to **one** of the questions (**7** or **8**) in this part.
Write your answer in about **100 words**.

Question 7

- This is part of a letter you receive from an English friend.

> *We're doing a school project about the environment. What environmental problems are there in your country? What can you tell me about recycling there?*

- Now write a **letter** to your friend.

Question 8

- Your English teacher has asked you to write a story.
- Your story must begin with this sentence:

    Diane saw a ring in the street and decided to pick it up.

- Write your **story**.

Students' own answers

LISTENING PART 1

Questions 1 – 7

There are seven questions in this part.
For each question, choose the correct answer **A**, **B** or **C**.

Example: What are they going to do?

Ⓐ

B

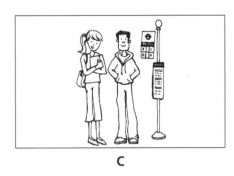

C

1 What present is the girl going to give her friend?

A

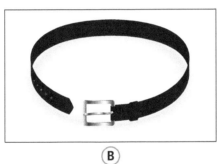

Ⓑ

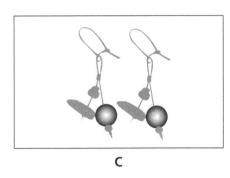

C

2 What will the weather be like today?

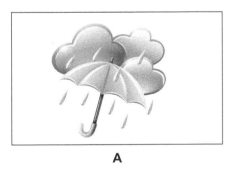

A

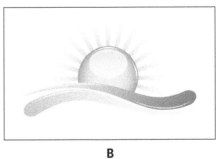

B

Ⓒ

3 Where was Janet last night?

Ⓐ

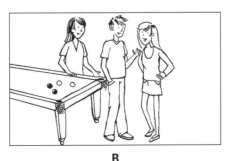

B

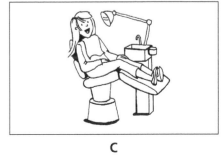

C

145

4 Which programme will be on before the news?

A B C

5 What do the students have to do at the art gallery?

  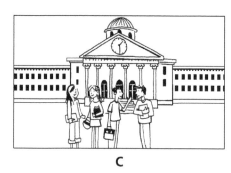

A B C

6 What does the boy order?

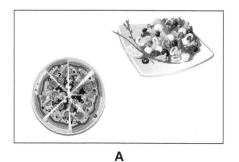  

A B C

7 What has Philip forgotten to take with him?

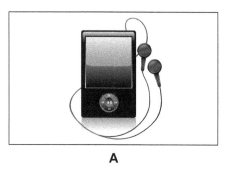  

A B C

LISTENING PART 2

Questions 8 – 13

You will hear an advertisement for a health club. For each question, choose the correct answer **A**, **B** or **C**.

8 This health club is

   A only for people who want to lose weight.

   B only for people who want to be stronger.

   C for anyone who wants to get and stay fit.

9 Who can a teenager go with from five to seven in the evening?

   A a parent

   B a friend

   C a personal trainer

10 What is Zumba, according to the advertisement?

   A a new type of dance

   B a new type of game

   C a new type of exercise

11 What can you buy at the shop?

   A things you may need for your sport

   B magazines about cooking

   C snacks and juices

12 The health club is encouraging young people to join by

   A giving them extra pocket money.

   B offering a low membership fee.

   C reducing the fee for their parents too.

13 With the special offer, a teenager can

   A go for a month for free.

   B pay £15 for six months.

   C get a discount of 50%.

LISTENING PART 3

Questions 14 – 19

You will hear some information about a history museum and an exhibition.
For each question, fill in the missing information in the numbered space.

THE HISTORY MUSEUM

Museum built: (14) _____ *1880* _____

Map of ancient world: dates and facts about each (15) _____ *country* _____

Leaflets: opening and closing times

EXHIBITIONS

Main feature: The (16) _____ *ancient Egypt* _____ collection

TUTANKHAMUN FACTS

Became king at the age of (17) _____ *nine/9* _____

Tomb was discovered by an (18) _____ *English* _____ archaeologist

Objects on display: jewellery, perfumed oils and
Tutankhamun's (19) _____ *mask* _____ (copy)

LISTENING PART 4

Questions 20 – 25

Look at the six sentences for this part.
You will hear a conversation between a girl, Celia, and a boy, Ryan, about a personal problem that Ryan has.
Decide if each sentence is correct or incorrect.
If it is correct, choose the letter **A** for **YES**. If it is not correct, choose the letter **B** for **NO**.

		YES	NO
20	Celia thinks that something bad has happened to Ryan.	(A)	B
21	Ryan wanted a smartphone.	(A)	B
22	Ryan's parents agreed to buy him the phone immediately.	A	(B)
23	Ryan paid for the phone by himself.	A	(B)
24	Ryan showed the new phone to his friend at school.	(A)	B
25	Ryan thinks his parents will understand the problem.	A	(B)

SPEAKING PART 1

2–3 minutes (3–4 minutes for a group of three)

Phase 1

This part is always the same. See page 30 of Test 1.

Phase 2
Interlocutor *(Select one or more questions from the list to ask each candidate. Use candidates' names throughout. Ask Candidate B first.)*

Tell us about your favourite school subject.
How much time do you spend doing homework?
What subject is the most difficult for you? Why?
What do you like about your school?
Would you like to be a teacher? Why?/Why not?
Thank you.

Introduction to Part 2
In the next part, you are going to talk to each other.

Students' own answers

SPEAKING PART 2

2–3 minutes (3 minutes for a group of three)

Best food and drinks for a picnic

Interlocutor
(Say to both candidates)

I'm going to describe a situation to you.
A group of friends want to go on a **picnic** in the park and they need to decide what **food and drinks** to take with them. Talk together about the **different** food and drinks they can **take** for the **picnic**. Then decide which food and drinks would be **best** for a **picnic**.
Here is a picture with some ideas to help you.

See pictures on page 181

I'll say that again.
A group of friends want to go on a **picnic** in the park and they need to decide what **food and drinks** to take with them. Talk together about the **different** food and drinks they can **take** for the **picnic**. Then decide which food and drinks would be **best** for a **picnic**.
All right? Talk together.

(Allow the candidates enough time to complete the task without intervention. Prompt only if necessary.)

Thank you.

Students' own answers

SPEAKING PART 3

3 minutes (4 minutes for a group of three)

Interlocutor *(Say to both candidates)*	Now, I'd like each of you to talk on your own about something. I'm going to give each of you a photograph of **tourists** who are on **sightseeing trips** in different places.
See photo A on page 182	*(Candidate A)*, here is your photograph. Please show it to *(Candidate B)*, but I'd like you to talk about it. *(Candidate B)*, you just listen. I'll give you your photograph in a moment. *(Candidate A)*, please tell us what you can see in your photograph.
Candidate A *(If there is a need to intervene, prompts rather than direct questions should be used.)*	*(Approximately 1 minute)*
Interlocutor See photo B on page 182	Thank you. Now, *(Candidate B)*, here is your photograph. It also shows **tourists** who are on a **sightseeing trip**. Please show it to *(Candidate A)* and tell us what you can see in the photograph.
Candidate B *(If there is a need to intervene, prompts rather than direct questions should be used.)*	*(Approximately 1 minute)*
Interlocutor	Thank you.

SPEAKING PART 4

3 minutes (3–4 minutes for a group of three)

Interlocutor *(Say to both candidates)*	Your photographs showed **tourists** on **sightseeing trips** in different places. Now, I'd like you to talk together about **sightseeing trips** that **you've been on** and the places where you'd **like** to go **sightseeing** in the **future**.

(Allow the candidates enough time to complete the task without intervention. Prompt only if necessary.)

Thank you. That's the end of the test.

Students' own answers

READING `PART 1`

Questions 1 – 5

Look at the text in each question.
What does it say?
Mark the correct letter **A**, **B** or **C**.

Example:

0

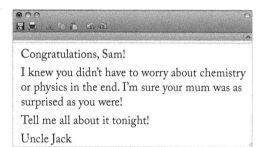

Congratulations, Sam!

I knew you didn't have to worry about chemistry or physics in the end. I'm sure your mum was as surprised as you were!

Tell me all about it tonight!

Uncle Jack

Who expected Sam to have problems in his exams?

A   only Sam

B   Sam's uncle

C   Sam and his mum

Answer: 0 

1

CHOC DRINK:
your favourite
chocolate drink

Sugar free – no artificial colours or flavours

Mix at least one spoon with water or milk. Drink immediately. Have up to 3 cups daily, best before meals. You'll see the difference in no time.

A   You mustn't have *Choc Drink* more than once a day.

B   You have to wait before you drink a cup of *Choc Drink*.

C   *Choc Drink* is a good choice if you're on a diet.

2

How to lift correctly

   Legs bent, keep back as straight as possible. Keep the object close to your body.

   Don't put all the weight on the muscles of your back.

Which piece of advice is correct?

A   Try not to bend your back very much.

B   Don't use your leg muscles to lift an object.

C   Hold the object at a distance.

3

Dad,

I'm at Carl's. I'll be back before 4pm, but I might not make it for lunch. I can't call you; no talk-time left on phone! Text me if you want anything from the shops.

Leo

A Leo's dad can send him a message if he needs to.

B If Leo needs something, he can text his dad.

C Leo's dad can have lunch with him before four o'clock.

4

REMEMBER

A SmartPark card is required to pay for daily parking.

SmartPark cards are only available online. Buy before April 30th and get 15% off.

A Buying a SmartPark card online is 15% cheaper in April.

B You must buy SmartPark cards in the car park.

C If you park in the car park every day, you don't need a card.

5

Sue, 6.04pm — What time tonight?

Natasha, 6.06pm — Film starts at 8. Pick me up at 7.15?

Sue, 6.11pm — OK. I'll ring the bell.

Natasha, 6.13pm — Don't forget to bring the jacket I lent you!

Sue, 6.14pm — I won't!

A Sue will give Natasha a ring when she gets to her house.

B Sue must remember to lend Natasha a jacket.

C Natasha reminds Sue about something she borrowed.

READING PART 2

Questions 6 – 10

The teenagers below are all looking for a music concert to go to.
On the opposite page, there are descriptions of eight concerts for young people.
Decide which concert would be the most suitable for the following teenagers.
For questions **6 – 10**, mark the correct letter (**A – H**).

6

Alexander, who enjoys listening to modern rock, wants to go to a rock concert with his sister. She isn't a big fan of electronic music, and she'd like to go to a rock concert that isn't too loud.

C

7

Ian likes concerts with a lot of instruments, but he isn't very keen on music from Central or South America. He likes modern and classical music and he'd prefer to see a concert in a big theatre.

B

8

Bridget, who is a big fan of the Beatles and rock and roll, finds unplugged concerts boring. She likes collecting souvenirs from the concerts she goes to.

E

9

Wesley is from the UK and he loves listening to music from other countries even though he doesn't understand the lyrics. He'd like to help other people in some way.

D

10

Vanessa is half Spanish. She usually likes watching ballet dancers perform, but this time she'd love to watch a big international star in concert.

F

Concerts

A **Charity Classics**
Come to the stadium this Thursday evening!
Enjoy the sound of the local symphony
orchestra. Don't miss this amazing classical
music performance live on stage. Be there at
7.30pm. All ticket sales go to *Save the Wildlife*.

B **Tchaikovksy's Swan Lake**
Professor David Elliot is bringing this
masterpiece alive to London's Grand Theatre.
Swan Lake will be played by the Middleton
student orchestra this weekend only. There
may be no ballet dancers, but the music will
make you want to dance. Tickets sold online.

C **Melina Brown unplugged**
18-year-old Melina Brown is on her way to
becoming a big rock star. She's performing
next Friday at the public youth club. Melina –
influenced by rock singers such as Kurt Cobain
and Mick Jagger – will play her own songs on
her acoustic guitar. Tickets are limited. Get
yours today!

D **Stars for Africa**
Paul Alwin of Radioheart and Julie Jones of
Heavenly 4 are joining forces for next month's
charity concert. They won't be singing their
big hits, but traditional African songs with
musicians from Senegal. Venue: Ben's Place.
Tickets: 18 euros (all money raised will go to
charity *Help Africa*).

E **Rock 'n Roll Robin**
American singer Robin King and his band are
playing tonight after 9pm in the main square.
All you Elvis Presley lovers must not miss it!
This is the best tribute band to the King of
Rock and Roll! T-shirts, CDs and posters will be
available next to the stage. It's now or never!

F **Marco Antonino**
He's been in the Latin music industry for
decades, but this is his first concert in London's
Wembley Stadium. Marco, the big salsa star,
will give six performances this August as part
of his world tour. His group of dancers and
musicians will amaze you! Don't wait any
longer to buy your ticket!

G **Mariziachi Band**
Are you tired of listening to the same kind
of music? If so, the Mariziachi Band is here
to cheer you up. Their sound is fresh, fun
and Mexican! Big hats, colourful suits, huge
guitars, violins and trumpets will guarantee
a great afternoon. Don't worry about not
understanding the Spanish lyrics; the rhythm
of the rancheras won't let you sit down!
5.30pm, Music Theatre

H **The Rhythmic Tigers**
'The Beatles' successors are in town,'
according to music producer Steve Richards.
The Rhythmic Tigers may remind you of the
Beatles, but their sound is unique. Electronic,
loud and experimental, the five Tigers from
London are presenting their new album at the
open air festival this Thursday, 9pm.

READING PART 3

Questions 11 – 20

Look at the sentences below about a famous hotel in Sweden.
Read the text on the opposite page to decide if each sentence is correct or incorrect.
If it is correct, mark **A**.
If it is not correct, mark **B**.

11	The Ice Hotel can be seen all year round in the north of Sweden.	A	(B)
12	The builders have to destroy the Ice Hotel each year at the end of April.	A	(B)
13	Everything in the Ice Hotel is made of either ice or snow.	(A)	B
14	Visitors who arrive in December will see the Ice Hotel before it's finished.	A	(B)
15	The website says the summer is a great time to visit the Ice Hotel.	A	(B)
16	There are only cold rooms available at the Ice Hotel itself.	(A)	B
17	The temperature in the Ice Hotel can be as cold as -10°C.	A	(B)
18	Visitors don't have to pay extra to stay warm at night.	(A)	B
19	The winter activities are only suitable for people who like adventure.	A	(B)
20	More people prefer to go rafting than fishing in the summer.	(A)	B

The coolest hotel in the world

About the Ice Hotel

The Ice Hotel, which is located in a small village in the north of Sweden, was built in 1990 for the first time. It is rebuilt each year from the middle of November because it starts to melt at the end of April. The whole hotel is made of – ice and snow! Every year a team of snow builders, architects, designers and artists gather to create this amazing hotel.

When to come

If you come at the beginning of winter, you'll be able to see parts of the hotel being built and artists sculpting huge blocks of ice. The warmer months of spring and summer are also a nice time to visit this area of Sweden – called Lapland – because night starts turning into day. This means the sun almost never sets. But, of course, if you come then, you won't be able to stay at the Ice Hotel!

Accommodation

You can choose to sleep in a warm room in a cabin or hotel nearby or a cold room in the Ice Hotel. The temperature inside the hotel doesn't go lower than -8°C. However, you'll need special clothes and a hat when you get into your sleeping bag. Warm winter clothes and other equipment are included in the price. In the rooms, the beds, furniture and sculptures are all made from ice!

Activities

If you like extreme activities, you can go on a snowmobile tour or discover the wild landscape on a sleigh pulled by dogs. If you're artistic, then why not try ice sculpting? And for those who are feeling romantic, the Northern Lights are an unforgettable sight. If you choose to come in summer, river rafting is the most popular activity. Some visitors also enjoy fishing in the Torne River.

READING PART 4

Questions 21 – 25

Read the text and questions below.
For each question, mark the correct letter **A**, **B**, **C** or **D**.

Are personal shoppers a growing fashion?

A day in the life of a personal shopper

'Personal shoppers are in great demand these days,' says Thomas, who has been working as one for the past five years. As we were walking past designer clothes shops, I asked him why he thinks this has happened. He says that there are many people who want to be fashionable, but they don't know where to start. They need a professional to advise them.

But why? I always call my best friend to help me find the perfect dress, not a stranger! 'I can help in three different ways. The first thing I do is help my customer improve their image. I teach them to choose colours and clothes that suit them, and how to use make-up,' Thomas tells me. 'Then I organise the customer's wardrobe; I might even throw away some old clothes.' The third service has to do with actual shopping: the personal shopper and the customer visit shops and buy clothes according to the customer's personality, lifestyle and needs.

Of course, each of the above services costs between 150 and 225 euros! Do many people have this kind of money to spend? 'Most of my customers are rich business people who call me for important meetings or business parties,' explains Thomas. 'However, I also work for people in all kinds of jobs and for retired men and women who want a change of look.' I was quite impressed, but I still didn't see why ordinary people would need someone like Thomas.

We spent the rest of the day shopping. Every time we came out of a shop, we had one more bag. In the end, I went home with a beautiful dress, two pairs of trousers, some lovely tops and a couple of coats. I'd never had a shopping day like this before! I admit that I'd spent more than I usually do, but I wouldn't have found such beautiful clothes without Thomas. I just wish personal shoppers were a bit cheaper!

21 What is the writer doing in the article?

    A talking about shopping in expensive shops

    B finding out what personal shoppers do

    C describing how she chooses which clothes to buy

    D explaining the kind of clothes Thomas buys

22 Why does Thomas think personal shoppers are mainly necessary?

    A People don't like following fashion.

    B People have started shopping for designer clothes.

    C People want to spend less money on clothes.

    D People need help with choosing the right clothes.

23 What does Thomas say about the services a personal shopper offers?

    A The customer can learn things through these services. .

    B The customer can't choose which service to pay for.

    C They don't depend on the customer's character and preferences.

    D The third service is more useful than the other two.

24 What was the writer's attitude to personal shopping?

    A She didn't understand why people wanted to look different.

    B She believed it was an important job.

    C She felt it wasn't essential.

    D She agreed that these services were necessary.

25 How might the writer describe her shopping day with Thomas?

A
An enjoyable day, and surprisingly cheap.

B
A fun day, but it ended badly.

C
An amazing day despite my doubts.

D
An unexpected day that wasn't worth the money.

READING PART 5

Questions 26 – 35

Read the text below and choose the correct word for each space.
For each question, mark the correct letter **A**, **B**, **C** or **D**.

Example:

0	A	to	B	for	C	of	D	at

Answer:

0	A	B	C	D
	■	▭	▭	▭

We're on the air in 4, 3, 2, 1!

Television is an exciting world **(0)** ___ be working in! Whether you **(26)** ___ to work as a TV presenter, a camera operator, a TV producer or in the lighting department, we have the advice and information **(27)** ___ you need. You **(28)** ___ not be sure yet what job interests you most, but we will help you to decide. Here are some tips before you **(29)** ___ up your mind.

Making a TV programme is not as simple as it may **(30)** ___. Many specialists working in different teams are necessary for a successful TV programme. Let's take the job of camera operators, for instance. **(31)** ___ being behind the camera, their work is essential. They have to know how to use different kinds of equipment, they're responsible **(32)** ___ setting up the cameras and they must know the script. It can also be a dangerous **(33)** ___ because they sometimes have to film scenes that involve fast-moving cars or explosions. Did you know that?

Check **(34)** ___ our website for more information about other jobs in television. Don't **(35)** ___ the documentary on the process of filming a TV programme, as well as interviews with famous TV presenters, producers and other professionals.

26	A	love	B	like	C	interest	D	want
27	A	who	B	that	C	when	D	what
28	A	must	B	should	C	might	D	can
29	A	take	B	make	C	give	D	do
30	A	seem	B	think	C	say	D	see
31	A	Even though	B	But	C	Despite	D	In spite
32	A	for	B	of	C	at	D	in
33	A	job	B	work	C	way	D	place
34	A	in	B	out	C	for	D	to
35	A	lose	B	catch	C	drop	D	miss

WRITING PART 1

Questions 1 – 5

Here are some sentences about housework.
For each question, complete the second sentence so that it means the same as the first.
Use no more than three words.
Write only the missing words.
You may use this page for any rough work.

Example:

0   It's no problem for me to make my bed.

I don't mind _____ my bed.

Answer: | 0 | *making* |

---

1   Today, Mum's angry because I still haven't tidied up my room.

Mum's angry today because I haven't tidied up my room _____ *yet* _____.

2   'Why don't you put your books away before you go to bed?' Mum asked.

'How about _____ *putting / you put* _____ your books away before you go to bed?' Mum suggested.

3   We don't have a dishwasher so we must do the washing-up by hand.

If we had a dishwasher, we wouldn't _____ *have to / need to* _____ do the washing-up by hand.

4   Luckily for us, my dad loves to wash the dishes.

Luckily for us, _____ *washing (the)* _____ dishes is my dad's favourite job at home.

5   Our washing machine really annoys me because it's very noisy.

Our washing machine is _____ *(really) annoying* _____ because it makes so much noise.

WRITING PART 2

Question 6

You are writing a school project about a famous person from the UK.

Write an email to your English friend. In your email, you should:

- explain what you have to do
- ask your friend to tell you about a famous person from the UK
- offer to send a copy of the finished project.

Write **35–45 words**.

Students' own answers

WRITING PART 3

Write an answer to **one** of the questions (**7** or **8**) in this part.
Write your answer in about **100 words**.

Question 7

- This is part of a letter you receive from an English friend.

> *I'm not feeling very well. I think I'm starting to get a cold. What should I do? Do I have to take medicine? Please tell me how to get well.*

- Now write a **letter** to your friend.

Question 8

- Your English teacher has asked you to write a story.
- Your story must begin with this sentence:

   Jim woke up, looked around and had no idea where he was.

- Write your **story**.

Students' own answers

LISTENING PART 1

Questions 1 – 7

There are seven questions in this part.
For each question, choose the correct answer **A**, **B** or **C**.

Example: What is the girl going to have?

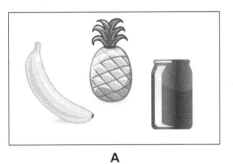

A

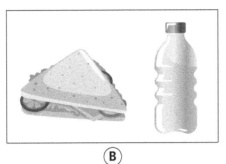

(B)

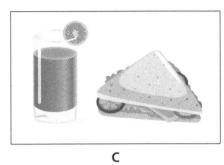

C

1 What is the girl going to take to the park?

(A)

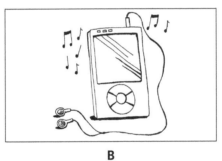

B

C

2 What did the singer like most?

A

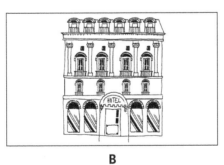

B

(C)

3 When will they go on holiday?

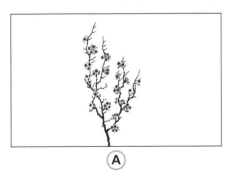

(A)

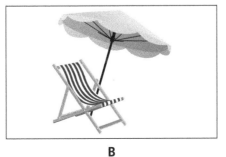

B

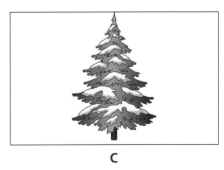

C

4 What exam does the teacher announce for Friday?

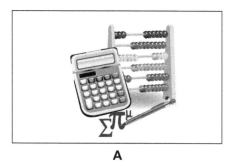

A

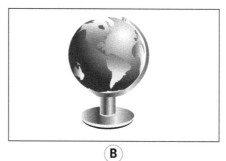

(B)

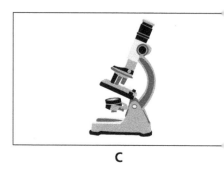

C

5 What time is it now?

A

(B)

C

6 What is the girl drinking?

A

B

(C)

7 Who is going to take the dog for a walk?

(A)

B

C

LISTENING `PART 2`

Questions 8 – 13

You will hear part of an interview with Stacey Peterson, a young designer who makes theatre costumes. For each question, choose the correct answer **A**, **B** or **C**.

8   How did Stacey start making costumes for the theatre?

    A A director liked one of her designs.

    B She used to work in a theatre.

    C A friend encouraged her to start.

9   According to Stacey, what's the best thing about her job?

    A It allows her to be very creative.

    B Famous actors wear her costumes on stage.

    C She doesn't work with the same people all the time.

10   Stacey is worried about the next play because

    A she has to make many costumes.

    B she will use a new material.

    C she has got little time to prepare.

11   How does Stacey get ideas for her costumes?

    A She surfs on the Internet.

    B She goes to fashion shows.

    C She borrows books from a library.

12   What would Stacey like to do in the future?

    A start designing something different

    B continue making costumes, but not for plays

    C teach students how to make clothes

13   Stacey advises anyone who wants to become a costume designer

    A to go to the theatre as much as possible.

    B to study fashion design at university.

    C to take photographs of clothes they like.

LISTENING PART 3

Questions 14 – 19

You will hear some advice on how to decorate your bedroom.
For each question, fill in the missing information in the numbered space.

How to decorate your bedroom

Before you start

Get rid of: (14) _____ *(old) toys* _____

Move furniture to: the (15) _____ *middle* _____ of the room

Choose: a (16) _____ *style* _____ for your room

Decorating

If you can't change things, be: (17) _____ *creative* _____

Avoid: very (18) _____ *bright* _____ and dark wall colours

In a corner, place a few: (19) _____ *(big) cushions* _____

LISTENING PART 4

Questions 20 – 25

Look at the six sentences for this part.
You will hear a conversation between a brother, Andy, and sister, Carol, about the weekend.
Decide if each sentence is correct or incorrect.
If it is correct, choose the letter **A** for **YES**. If it is not correct, choose the letter **B** for **NO**.

		YES	NO
20	Andy has to study for an exam this weekend.	(A)	B
21	Carol wants to borrow Andy's laptop.	A	(B)
22	Andy and Carol agree to go to the cinema together.	A	(B)
23	Carol thinks they should help in the house more.	(A)	B
24	Andy suggests making breakfast on Sunday.	A	(B)
25	Carol plans to buy some vegetables for her salad.	(A)	B

SPEAKING PART 1

2–3 minutes (3–4 minutes for a group of three)

Phase 1

This part is always the same. See page 30 of Test 1.

Phase 2
Interlocutor *(Select one or more questions from the list to ask each candidate. Use candidates' names throughout. Ask Candidate B first.)*

Tell us about your home.
What's your favourite room in your home? Why?
What would you like to change in your home? Why?
What housework do you do to help at home?
Do you think it's better to live in a house or a flat? Why?
Thank you.

Introduction to Part 2
In the next part, you are going to talk to each other.

Students' own answers

SPEAKING PART 2

2–3 minutes (3 minutes for a group of three)

Best place to stay on a school trip

Interlocutor
(Say to both candidates)

I'm going to describe a situation to you.
A group of students are organising a **summer school trip**. They are going to a Spanish town by the **sea**, but they don't know where to stay. Talk together about the different **types of accommodation** and then decide which is the **most fun for the students to stay in**.

See pictures on page 183

Here is a picture with some ideas to help you.

I'll say that again.
A group of students are organising a **summer school trip**. They are going to a Spanish town by the **sea**, but they don't know where to stay. Talk together about the different **types of accommodation** and then decide which is the **most fun for the students to stay in**.
All right? Talk together.

(Allow the candidates enough time to complete the task without intervention. Prompt only if necessary.)

Thank you.

Students' own answers

SPEAKING PART 3

3 minutes (4 minutes for a group of three)

Interlocutor *(Say to both candidates)*	Now, I'd like each of you to talk on your own about something. I'm going to give each of you a photograph of **astronauts**.
See photo A on page 184	*(Candidate A)*, here is your photograph. Please show it to *(Candidate B)*, but I'd like you to talk about it. *(Candidate B)*, you just listen. I'll give you your photograph in a moment. *(Candidate A)*, please tell us what you can see in your photograph.
Candidate A	*(Approximately 1 minute)*
(If there is a need to intervene, prompts rather than direct questions should be used.)	
Interlocutor	Thank you. Now, *(Candidate B)*, here is your photograph. It also shows **astronauts**.
See photo B on page 184	Please show it to *(Candidate A)* and tell us what you can see in the photograph.
Candidate B	*(Approximately 1 minute)*
(If there is a need to intervene, prompts rather than direct questions should be used.)	
Interlocutor	Thank you.

SPEAKING PART 4

3 minutes (3–4 minutes for a group of three)

Interlocutor *(Say to both candidates)*	Your photographs showed **astronauts**. Now I'd like you to talk together about the **advantages and disadvantages** of being an astronaut and whether **you** would **like to be one**.

(Allow the candidates enough time to complete the task without intervention. Prompt only if necessary.)

Thank you. That's the end of the test.

Students' own answers

SPEAKING PART 2

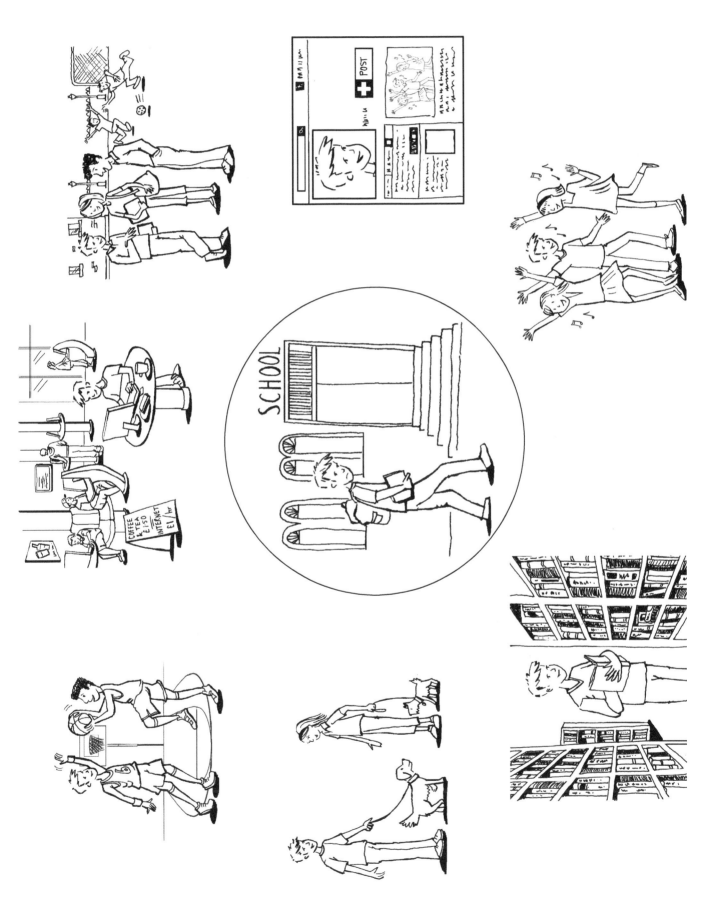

SPEAKING PART 3

Photograph for Candidate A

Photograph for Candidate B

SPEAKING PART 2

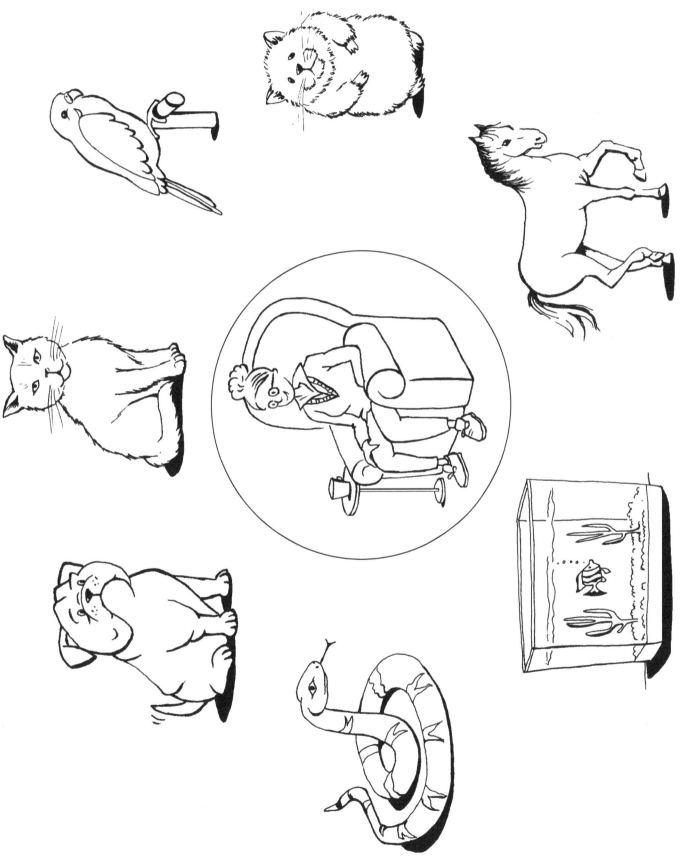

SPEAKING PART 3

Photograph for Candidate A

Photograph for Candidate B

SPEAKING PART 2

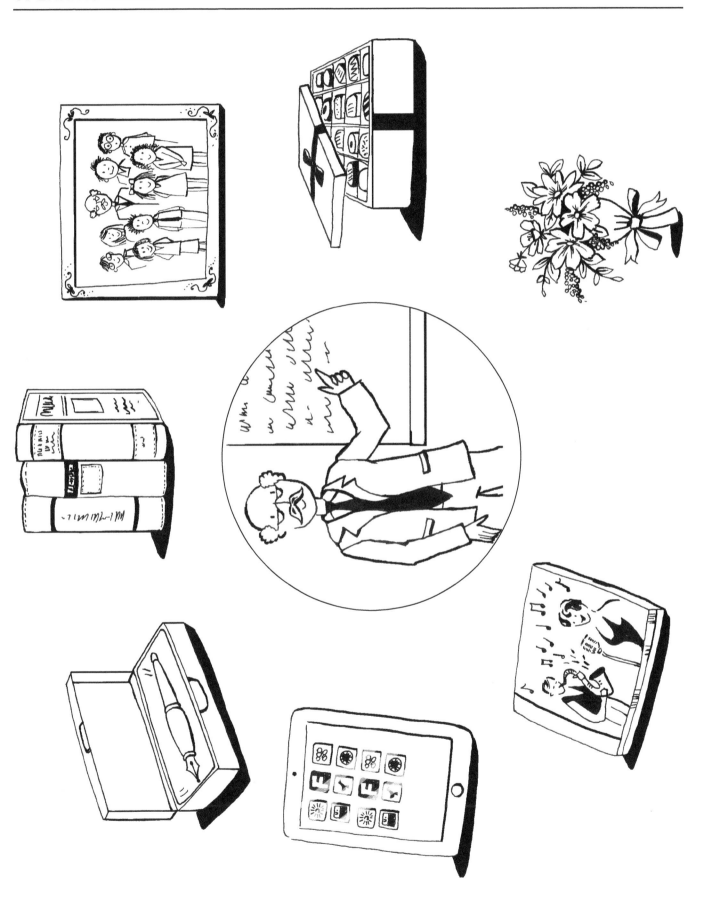

SPEAKING PART 3

Photograph for Candidate A

Photograph for Candidate B

SPEAKING PART 2

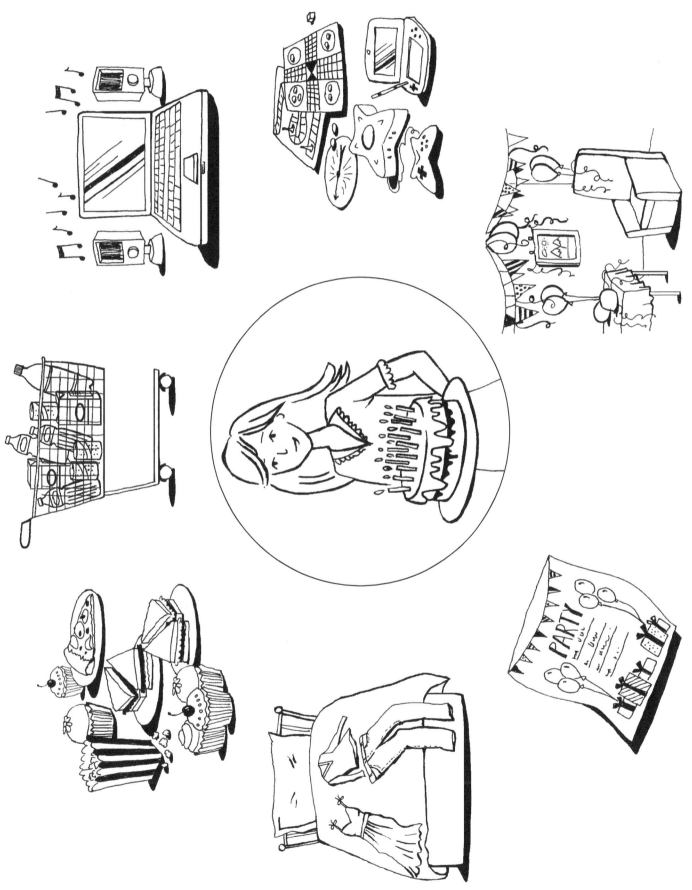

SPEAKING PART 3

Photograph for Candidate A

Photograph for Candidate B

SPEAKING PART 2

SPEAKING PART 3

Photograph for Candidate A

Photograph for Candidate B

SPEAKING PART 2

SPEAKING PART 3

Photograph for Candidate A

Photograph for Candidate B

SPEAKING PART 2

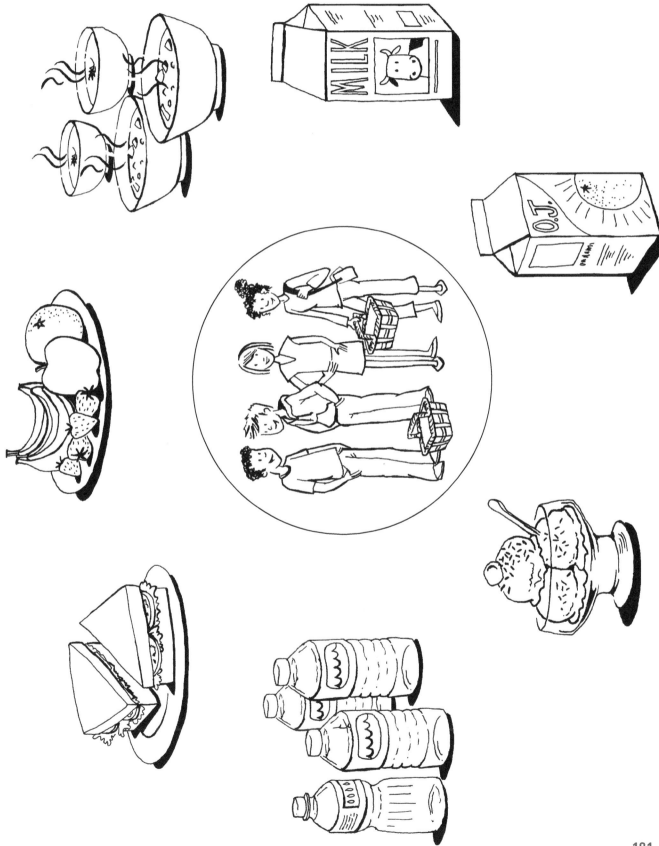

SPEAKING PART 3

Photograph for Candidate A

Photograph for Candidate B

SPEAKING PART 2

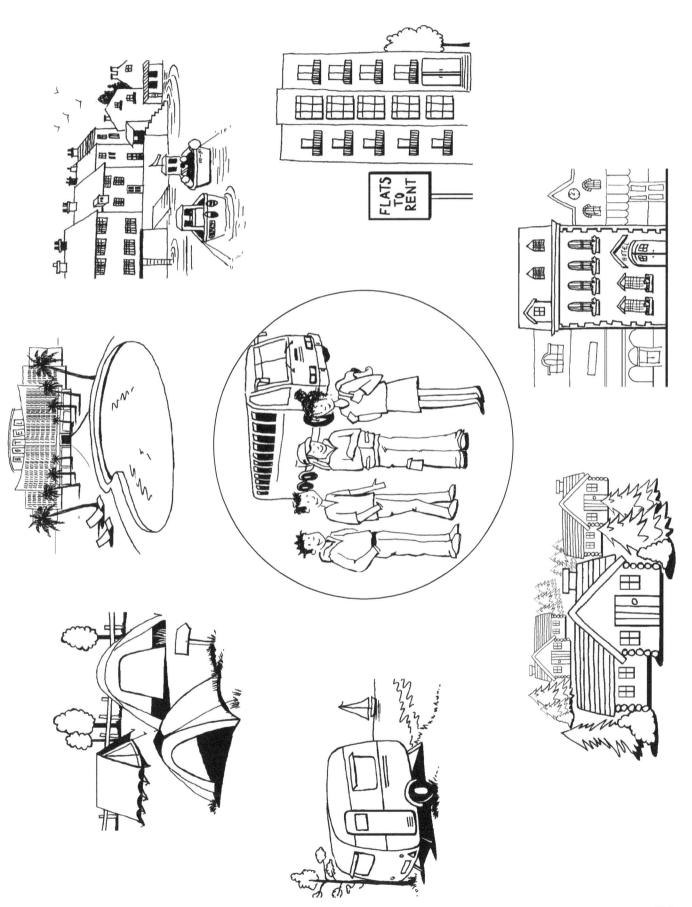

SPEAKING PART 3

Photograph for Candidate A

Photograph for Candidate B

Glossary

Practice Test 1

Reading Part 1

racket (n) the thing you hit the ball with in a sport like tennis

remind (v) tell someone something they might have forgotten

glue (n) sticky substance used to join things together

suitable (adj) safe or right

set (n) group of similar things

path (n) small road for people to walk on

lead (n) kind of rope or a chain tied to the collar of a dog

Reading Part 2

take up (phr v) begin a hobby or sport

be keen on (expr) be enthusiastic about

landscape (n) painting of the countryside

take place (expr) happen

instrument (n) something you use to make music, such as a piano

lyrics (n pl) words of songs

wildlife (n) living things in nature

protect (v) keep safe, look after

attend (v) go to and take part in

period (n) length of time

gallery (n) building where art is shown

chef (n) trained cook

come out (phr v) show

cuisine (n) style of cooking

traditional (adj) done in the same way by a group of people for a long time

dish (n) food prepared in a particular way

youngster (n) young person

recipe (n) instructions for how to prepare and cook food

ingredient (n) something that is added with other foods to make something to eat

nutritious (adj) full of healthy things

organisation (n) group of people who work together for a shared purpose

environment (n) the air, water and land, when we think of them as one

pollution (n) anything (especially a chemical) which makes the air, water or land dirty or poisonous

poles (n) very cold areas at the top and bottom of the Earth

generation (n) the people of about the same age within a family or society

opportunity (n) chance to do something

mysterious (adj) strange and hard to explain

exist (v) live

desert (n) large area where there is very little rain

valley (n) area of low land between hills or mountains

play a part in (expr) be an active part of an event

habitat (n) place where animals live

rhythm (n) musical beat

small-scale (adj) made like a real object, but smaller

aircraft (n) plane or helicopter

vessel (n) a ship or boat

fascinating (adj) very interesting

arrange (v) organise

pleasant (adj) nice

Reading Part 3

baggy (adj) not tight

uncomfortable (adj) too tight or heavy to wear, not comfortable

adult (n) someone over eighteen years old

manage to (v) be able to

opinion (n) what somebody thinks of something

cheap (adj) at a low price; not expensive

dress (v) wear clothes

cool (adj) fashionable, very good

popular (adj) liked by a lot of people

appear (v) be seen

wave (n) raised line of water in the sea

plenty (pron) a lot

neighbourhood (n) the local area

urban (adj) to do with the city

trainers (n) sports shoes

cap (n) type of hat

flexible (adj) allowing the wearer to move easily

casual (adj) not formal, in an everyday style

trendy (adj) in fashion

brand (n) the maker's name on products

accessory (n) something added to clothes which is useful or decorative, such as a bag or hat

plain (adj) with one colour and no decoration

can't afford (expr) not have enough money for

second-hand (adj) not new, already used by someone else

try out (phr v) do or use something to see if it works for you

copycat (n) someone who copies exactly what others have done

Glossary

Reading Part 4
habit (n) something you usually do
affect (v) cause something/somebody to change in some way
refuse (v) say you won't do something
snack (n) small meal
serve (v) offer as a choice of meal
put on weight (expr) get heavier
continue (v) go on, not stop
encourage (v) say something positive to help somebody do something
strict diet (expr) careful eating plan
regular (adj) happening often
proper (adj) correct
pay attention to (expr) think about

Reading Part 5
move in (phr v) go and stay for a long time in a house
employer (n) someone who gives people jobs
colleague (n) someone you work with
similar to (expr) like
reserve (v) keep
upper-class (adj) from the top (usually rich) level in society
youth (n) teenager or young adult
battle (n) fight
bow (n) weapon for shooting arrows
arrow (n) long thin pointed stick, usually with feathers at one end, that is shot from a bow
consider (v) think

Listening Part 2
audience (n) people who watch something
comfortable (adj) feeling relaxed
competition (n) an event where you try to win against others
sore (adj) painful
throat (n) the front or inside part of the neck
calm (adj) relaxed, peaceful

Listening Part 3
tracksuit (n) trousers and a matching top worn when doing sports
roller skates (n) skates with wheels
souvenir (n) something you keep as a reminder of a place or an event

Listening Part 4
several (adv) some
awful (adj) very bad

Practice Test 2

Reading Part 1
flat (n) apartment
central heating (n) system that warms the whole home
available (adj) ready to be used
public transport (expr) ways for people to travel together, for example, buses
pick up (phr v) collect, take from a place
diving (n) swimming under water
equipment (n) things needed for a particular purpose
fill out (phr v) write information
form (n) an official paper
boil (v) warm water until it reaches its hottest point
pan (n) round metal container used for cooking
stir (v) move something around
occasionally (adv) sometimes, not often
strainer (n) kind of bowl with holes in it to separate water from food
heat (v) make something hot
mix (v) put ingredients together
put somebody's name down for (expr) add somebody's name to a list to take part in something
document (n) piece of paper with written information
boarding pass (n) the card you need to get onto a plane or ship
flight (n) journey by plane
hold on to (phr v) keep
suit (n) set of matching jacket and trousers
dry cleaner's (n) shop where people take clothes for a special kind of cleaning
appointment (n) an arranged meeting

Reading Part 2
outdoor (adj) outside
facilities (n pl) services or buildings offered for a special use
located (adj) in a certain position
cycling (n) riding a bicycle
route (n) way to get from one place to another

hiking (n) walking long distances in the countryside
challenging (adj) difficult to do
make the most of (expr) take advantage of opportunities
range (n) group of things to choose from
set (adj) located, positioned
benefit from (v) have the advantage of
in the open air (expr) outside
huge (adj) very big
indoor (adj) inside
run (v) organise
woods (n pl) forest
woodland (n) an area with a lot of trees
creature (n) animal
owl (n) bird that flies at night and hunts small animals
bat (n) small flying animal with big ears which is active at night
badger (n) black and white animal which lives underground and comes out to feed at night
feature (n) important part
situated (adj) located
it's a must (expr) it's something you have to do or see
inspiration (n) something that gives you ideas or encouragement to do something
daily (adj) every day
session (n) organised period of time
field (n) open area of land
just (adv) simply
programme (n) an organised set of events
extreme (adj) testing to the limits
the latest (adj) the most recent
tent (n) the thing you live in when you go camping

Reading Part 3
appeal (v) be liked
locally (adv) in a small area
limited (adj) small in number
unsociable (adj) not wanting to be with other people, unfriendly
elsewhere (adv) in other places
hit (v) appear on
combine (v) put different things together, mix
mission (n) job, plan
interact (v) communicate
purpose (n) reason
team up with (phr v) join together to work as a team
enemy (n) person or group you fight against
pitch (n) an area for sports such as football
set up (phr v) arrange, make possible
have something in common (expr) have the same ideas and/or interests

stick to (phr v) stay with
log on (phr v) fill in a name and code to get onto a website
role playing (n) pretending to be somebody else
support (v) allow something to work
socialise (v) meet with other people
engage with (phr v) communicate with
otherwise (adv) if that doesn't happen
despite (prep) although it has

Reading Part 4
syndrome (n) medical problem
swear (v) use rude words
bad language (expr) rude way of talking
symptom (n) the sign of an illness
childhood (n) the state of being a child
tic (n) an uncontrollable quick movement
sharp (adj) quick
facial (adj) to do with the face
jerk (v) make a short sudden movement
pretty (adj) quite
embarrassing (adj) making someone feel uncomfortable
self-conscious (adj) too aware of your actions
cure (n) medical treatment to make someone well
medication (n) medicines, drugs
mild (adj) not strong
case (n) one example of a disease
coughing (n) forcing air out through your throat with a loud sound
sniffing (n) taking air in through your nose noisily
blinking (n) closing both your eyes quickly several times
suffer (v) feel ill or uncomfortable
uneasy (adj) not feeling comfortable
mind (v) care about

Reading Part 5
animation (n) moving drawings on film
hit (n) something that is a success
take off (phr v) become successful or popular
step (n) movement forwards
dwarf (dwarfs/dwarves) (n) very small person
release (v) make something, such as a film, available to the public
dozen (n) group of twelve
definitely (adv) for sure
discover (v) find out something that nobody else knew about
invent (v) make something that nobody has made before

Glossary

Writing Part 2
celebrate (v) do something to have fun together at a special time
invite (v) ask somebody to come to an event

Listening Part 2
documentary (n) TV programme or film about a true subject
expert (n) someone who knows a lot about a subject
complicated (adj) difficult to do or understand
topic (n) subject
image (n) picture

Listening Part 3
seat (v) give a place to sit down
wooden (adj) made of wood
lead (v) show the way to somewhere
wooded (adj) with many trees
robes (n pl) formal clothes

Listening Part 4
coming (adj) going to happen soon
present (adj) that is in use now

Speaking Part 2
elderly (adj) old (person)

Speaking Part 3
gadget (n) small device or machine with a particular purpose

Practice Test 3

Reading Part 1
Zumba (n) dance-fitness programme originally from South America
aerobics (n) kind of energetic exercise
give it a try (expr) try something for the first time
throw a party (expr) have a party
beginner (n) someone who has just started to learn how to do something

Reading Part 2
light (adj) not serious
romance (n) love
heartache (n) feelings of great sadness
recognise (v) remember a person or place
wonder (v) think about
fall to pieces (expr) lose control of your mind or feelings
run into (phr v) meet, have
teammate (n) someone on the same team
rather (adj) quite
fall in love with (expr) become romantically involved with
handsome (adj) good-looking (usually used for a man)
neighbour (n) someone who lives near your home
can't stand (v) hate, dislike
notice (v) see, pay attention to
fail (v) not manage to do something
give in (phr v) surrender, stop fighting
at one point (prep phr) at one moment
novel (n) book with a story
defend (v) protect from danger
feel sorry for (expr) feel sad about
for good (prep phr) for ever
split up (phr v) end a relationship
take an interest in (expr) become interested in
give up (phr v) stop trying
cure (v) make (something/someone) well
amusing (adj) a little bit funny
far from it (expr) quite different to what was said before
cruel (adj) hurtful
behind somebody's back (expr) without somebody knowing

decorations (n pl) things you put in a place to make it look nice

Reading Part 3
luxury (n) great comfort
coast (n) land next to the sea
resort (n) place where people go on holiday
aim at (phr v) design for
beforehand (adv) earlier than a previous time
lagoon (n) area of sea like a small lake, nearly separated from the sea
magnificent (adj) wonderful

sparkling (adj) bright
unique (adj) that has nothing else like it
memorable (adj) easy to remember, hard to forget
board (n) accommodation
antique (adj) something made in an earlier period and valued because it is old or of high quality
original (adj) not a copy
organic (adj) naturally grown without chemicals
for all tastes (expr) to suit everybody
lush (adj) with lots of plants
rolling hills (n) series of low hills
sunbathing (n) lying in the sun
rare (adj) not easily found, not common
enthusiast (n) someone who is very keen on a subject or activity
arts (n pl) the showing or doing of creative activities such as painting, acting, dancing and music
crafts (n pl) skills needed to make objects, particularly by hand
woodwork (n) making things by hand with wood
pottery (n) the skill of making pots by hand
neighbouring (adj) nearby, close
scuba diving (n) swimming underwater using an oxygen tank
rafting (n) water activity using a flat boat
theme park (n) large area for entertainment such as Disneyland
water slide (n) something in a water park which people have fun on by sliding down into the water
endless (adj) going on forever
at every step (expr) all the time
nesting ground (n) area where birds make nests to lay eggs
advise (v) give advice to somebody, suggest
brochure (n) an advertising magazine with pictures and information

Reading Part 4
counselling (n) giving advice or help, usually with social or personal problems
unthinkable (adj) too shocking or unlikely to think about
openly (adv) honestly and freely
service (n) system or organisation which offers some kind of help
counsellor (n) someone trained to give advice or help about personal problems
under pressure (prep phr) being stressed, usually when you have to do something that you don't have enough time for or don't want to do
face (v) have to deal with
economic (adj) to do with money
unemployment (n) the state of not having a job

push to the limits (expr) push as hard as possible
at some stage (prep phr) at some time
point of view (expr) opinion
in confidence (prep phr) with a promise that no one else will be told, in secret
adolescent (n) young person at the age between being a child and an adult
oblige (v) force, make someone do something
in the first place (expr) firstly, most importantly
identify (v) find out, name
learning disability (n) problem that stops people learning as well as they could
assist (v) help
guardian (n) someone who is responsible for a child when their natural parents aren't able to be
trivial (adj) not important
supportive (adj) practically helpful
express (v) show
nowadays (adv) these days, around now
out of work (prep phr) unemployed, without a job

Reading Part 5
hurricane (n) very strong wind that has a circular movement
tropical (adj) with hot wet weather
storm (n) extreme weather with strong wind and rain
ocean (n) very large area of sea
equator (n) the imaginary line around the centre of the Earth
first aid kit (n) box of things you might need to help someone who has an accident
forecast (n) prediction
flooded (adj) full of water
injured (adj) hurt
trapped (adj) not being able to get out of a place
tap water (n) water that you get from the tap in your kitchen and bathroom
rescue (v) save, help someone out of a dangerous situation
slightly (adv) a bit

Writing Part 1
cooker (n) machine for cooking food
careless (adj) not careful
safety rules (n pl) list of rules that give advice on how to do something safely

Writing Part 3
carnival (n) special time of year in some countries when people celebrate in the streets

Glossary

Listening Part 2

raise money (v) try to get money for a particular reason

charity (n) an organisation that works to help others

candle (n) thin thing that slowly burns as it gives light. You often put candles on birthday cakes and blow them out

pocket money (n) the small amounts of money parents give their children

Listening Part 4

vegetarian (n) someone who doesn't eat meat or fish

Practice Test 4

Reading Part 1

Big Ben (n) the bell in the famous clock tower in central London

queue (n) line of waiting people

the London Eye (n) the big wheel in the centre of London that people can pay to ride on to have a view of the city

eat out (phr v) have a meal outside your home, for example, in a restaurant

bin (n) container for rubbish

sunglasses (n pl) glasses you wear to protect your eyes from the sun

(20%) off (expr) (20%) cheaper than the earlier price of an item

original (adj) first

recycle (v) collect and use old things or rubbish to be used again or made into something else

helmet (n) hard hat to protect your head

tyre (n) outside part of a wheel made of rubber which goes on a bike or car

surfboard (n) long, thin thing that you can take into the sea and stand on to ride waves

wetsuit (n) tight-fitting waterproof piece of clothing you wear to keep you warm in the water

resit (v) take an exam again because you failed or didn't get a good mark before

secretary (n) someone who works in an office and helps organise and arrange things

term (n) fixed period of time, for example, a part of the school year

with regards (prep phr) polite way to end a letter or email to say with best wishes

Reading Part 2

mystery (n) something which is unexplained or unknown

solve (v) find the answer to a difficult or mysterious problem

puzzle (n) problem or question that you have to solve by using your mind

space (n) the empty area outside the Earth's atmosphere where the stars and planets are

fan (n) someone who is very enthusiastic about a particular thing

science fiction (n) stories and films about an imagined future

cheerful (adj) happy

intense (adj) causing very strong feelings

figure-skating (n) ice-skating that tries to be as beautiful as possible

single (adj) one

episode (n) one programme in a TV series

hunt down (phr v) try to catch

twin (n) one of two children born to the same mother at the same time

scary (adj) frightening

alien (n) creature not from Earth

get rid of (phr v) throw out, make go away

on their way (prep phr) coming

tune in (phr v) turn on the TV and watch a programme

anti- (prefix) opposed to, against

duo (n) two people who work together as a team

detective (n) someone who tries to find out information about a crime

actually (adv) in reality

unwelcoming (adj) unfriendly

set (n) the furniture and other things that are made or built to show the place where a film or play happens

subtitles (n pl) translation of a film script into another language which you can read at the bottom of the screen while watching

knight (n) man in the past who had an important position and fought enemies while riding a horse

monster (n) huge or unnatural creature

wizard (n) man with power to do magic

theme song (n) the song that is played at the beginning or end of a TV series by which you can recognise the programme

award (n) prize

girlie (adj) suitable for girls

break someone's heart (expr) hurt someone's feelings badly by stopping a romantic relationship

plot (n) the story of a book or film

be into (phr v) be very interested in

musical (n) film or stage show with singing and often dancing

on stage (prep phr) performing in a theatre or other place of entertainment in front of an audience

rock (v) excite

Reading Part 3

store (v) keep in a safe place

soap (n) something you can clean yourself with

routine (n) set of actions you do regularly as a habit

Good for you! (expr) Well done!

yoghurt (n) food made from milk sometimes with pieces of fruit in it

cupboard (n) piece of furniture with doors and shelves where you store things

jar (n) glass thing to keep food in

gift (n) present

method (n) way of doing something

running (adj) moving

guide (n) written advice or instructions on how to do something

Reading Part 4

exhausted (adj) very tired

wide awake (adj) not at all sleepy

temple (n) building where people meet for religious ceremonies

bazaar (n) an area of small shops and people selling things

unbelievable (adj) very surprising

constant (adj) happening very often or all the time

passenger (n) someone who is travelling on a means of transport and who is not the driver

suitcase (n) bag you pack things in when you are going on a journey

luggage (n) all the bags you carry with you on a journey

straight (adv) immediately, without waiting

powder (n) very small pieces of a substance, such as flour

perfume (n) nice-smelling liquid often made from flower oils

click away (phr v) take many photos one after the other

water pistol (n) toy gun that shoots water

annoyed (adj) angry

destroy (v) damage something completely so that it can't be used anymore

Reading Part 5

the underground (n) the metro, the underground train system

vehicle (n) something people use to travel around in, such as a car or bus

symbol (n) something which represents something else

capital (n) the most important city in a country

zoom (v) move quickly

Listening Part 2

journalist (n) someone who writes articles for a newspaper or magazine or reports for a TV or radio station

greetings card (n) card you send to someone on a special occasion, such as a birthday

heights (n pl) high places

sunset (n) time of day when the sun goes down and it begins to get dark

Practice Test 5

Reading Part 1

on (adv) happening

off (adv) not at work

sick (adj) ill, not well

receipt (n) piece of paper which shows you have paid for something

refund (n) money that is returned to you

exchange (n) changing of one thing for something else of a similar value or type

prove (v) show that something is really true

note (v) notice, pay attention to

platform (n) place in a railway station where you get on a train

gate (n) entrance where your tickets may be checked

make it (expr) arrange something

brake (n) device that can make a vehicle go slower or stop

repairs (n pl) what you do to make something that is damaged work again

customer (n) someone who buys something from a shop

Reading Part 2

invention (n) something which has never been made before

try out (phr v) do or use for the first time

design (n) plan for the shape and style of clothes, etc.

costume (n) set of clothes worn for a particular activity or to show an identity

Glossary

fancy dress party (n) party to which you wear strange or unusual clothes
classical (adj) traditional
sculpture (n) work of art made of materials such as wood, metal or stone
ancient (adj) thousands of years old
war (n) long period of fighting between different groups – often countries
exhibition (n) public show
in years gone by (expr) in the past
archaeologist (n) someone who studies the things of people who lived in the past
public bath (n) place where people can swim or relax in water together
statue (n) object made of a hard material to look like a person or animal
sculptor (n) someone who makes sculptures
on display (prep phr) in a special area where people can see it
operate (v) use a machine
exhibit (n) something that is shown publically
diagram (n) technical drawing
on sale (prep phr) available to buy
demonstrate (v) show how something works or happens
try on (phr v) wear something to see if it is suitable
scientific (adj) to do with science
discovery (n) finding something for the first time
laboratory (n) place where scientists do practical work

Reading Part 3
permanent (adj) always there, not just for a short period
company (n) an organisation that tries to make money
in charge of (prep phr) responsible for, organising
permission (n) document or statement that allows somebody to do something
earn (v) get money by working
season (n) period of time, usually spring, summer, autumn or winter
link (n) connection on the Internet
post (v) put a message on a website
CV (n) Curriculum Vitae; a list of your qualifications and experience that you can send when you apply for a job
local (adj) nearby, close to home
dog-walking (n) job which is taking people's dogs for walks

staff (n) all the people who work in a place
in touch (prep phr) in contact
help out (phr v) help when something particular needs to be done
community centre (n) place where people from an area can meet and do activities
assistant (n) someone who helps someone else to do a job
pick (v) collect
adventurous (adj) brave and wanting to try something new or dangerous
foreign (adj) in or from another country

Reading Part 4
eco-friendly (adj) not damaging the environment
prevent (v) stop something from happening
replace (v) put one thing where something else was
light bulb (n) an electric light
solar (adj) to do with the sun
panel (n) thin, flat thing that fits onto something else
roof (n) the top of a house
bill (n) request for payment for things like electricity and water
employ (v) give someone a job
in a mess (prep phr) mixed up, not organised
ceiling (n) top part of a room which you can see when you look up
switch (n) something you touch on the wall to make the lights go on/off
motion detector (n) something that knows when there is movement
switch off (phr v) turn off something that works from electricity
automatically (adv) by itself without needing anybody to touch it
regret (v) feel sorry for what happened in the past
glad (adj) happy
that's what matters (expr) that's what is important

Reading Part 5
mammal (n) animal that gives birth to babies which feed from their mother's milk
whale (n) very large sea mammal
breathe (v) take air into the body and let it out
breath (n) air that you take in and let out of your body
shallow (adj) not deep
particularly (adv) especially, mostly

Listening Part 2
climate (n) general weather conditions in a place
suit (v) be suitable or right for
sausage (n) meat mixed with other ingredients and made into a long thin shape

Listening Part 3
announcement (n) something said for everyone to hear
delay (n) lateness in something happening
terminal (n) the part of an airport where planes leave from or arrive at
security (n) safeness

Listening Part 4
essential (adj) completely necessary

Practice Test 6

Reading Part 1
puppy (n) young dog
playful (adj) lively, enjoying playing
let someone know (expr) tell someone about something
bowling (n) game in which you roll a heavy ball down a track to try and knock down wooden objects
cancel (v) decide that an arranged event or meeting will not happen
library (n) building or room where books are kept and might be borrowed
playground (n) an outdoor space at a school where children can play
in peace (prep phr) without noise around
borrow (v) take something from someone for a time and then give it back later
lake (n) large area of fresh water
sign up (phr v) write your name on a list in order to do a course/activity
register (v) put your name on a list in order to do a course/activity

Reading Part 2
penfriend (n) someone you write to who you have usually never met
British (adj) from England, Scotland, Wales or Northern Ireland
culture (n) the way of life in particular places

photography (n) the skill or activity of taking and producing photographs
download (v) move information from the Internet to your computer
sporty (adj) being good at or enjoying doing sports
normally (adv) usually
busy (adj) having lots of things to do, with no free time
out and about (expr) away from your home
milk (v) take milk from an animal such as a cow
feed (v) give food to
look after (phr v) take care of, protect
dirty (adj) not clean
count (v) include
drive someone crazy (expr) make someone upset or angry

Reading Part 3
fair (n) exhibition
present (v) show what you have done
variety (n) range of different things
practical (adj) useful
experience (n) something you do, see or feel that has an effect on you
be packed with (expr) be full of
impressed (adj) thinking something was good
show off (phr v) proudly present what you have done
volcano (n) mountain with a hole at the top through which hot substances can be forced out
wind farm (n) an area that produces electricity from the wind
cardboard (n) material like very thick paper often used to make boxes
pick (v) choose
steam (n) gas created when you boil water
power (v) make something work with a source of energy
effective (adj) working well
feel proud of (expr) feel happy about something
achieve (v) succeed in finishing something
experiment (v) try doing something to see if it is possible
text book (n) book written for students to learn about a subject
workshop (n) meeting to discuss or do practical activities
drama (n) theatre
historic (adj) in the past and important
remain (v) stay
hall (n) large indoor space
all in all (expr) considering everything, in summary

Glossary

Reading Part 4

private (adj) personal, not for the use of everyone
long-lost friend (n) friend you have lost contact with and then find again
pass the time (expr) spend free time
bowling alley (n) the place where you can go bowling
brilliant (adj) great, excellent
professional (adj) to do with work
business (n) company or organisation which buys and sells things
comment (n) an opinion
rude (adj) not polite or kind, hurtful
unfair (adj) not fair, not right
nasty (adj) not nice, bad
warn (v) say that something is dangerous
persuade (v) make someone believe something is true
confusing (adj) not easy to understand, mixed up in the mind
mainly (adv) mostly
resource (n) something that is useful to help you do something
behave (v) act in a certain way

Reading Part 5

gymnastics (n) physical exercises usually done inside
when it comes to (expr) concerning, about (a subject)
handball (n) team sport in which you score by throwing a ball into a goal
motocross (n) sport in which people ride specially-designed motorbikes over rough ground, not on roads

Listening Part 2

dining room (n) the room where you eat
detention (n) having to stay longer after classes at school because you have done something bad

Listening Part 3

temperature (n) measure of how hot something is
degree (n) unit of measurement of temperature; for example, water boils at 100 degrees Celsius
cocoa (n) the dark brown powder used to make chocolate

teaspoon (n) small spoon that is usually used for stirring milk and sugar in a cup of tea or coffee
baking powder (n) mix of powders used to make cakes rise and become light when they are baked
bake (v) cook in a cooker without any liquid or fat

Practice Test 7

Reading Part 1

oven (n) the inside part of a cooker
PS (abbr) postscript; written to add extra text at the end of a letter after signing your name
call back (phr v) telephone someone who called you when you were not available
jog (n) a slow run
application (n) app, an extra useful thing you can add to your smartphone or computer
lab (abbr) laboratory
court (n) a place to play sports such as tennis and basketball
sweater (n) item of clothing which you can wear on the top half of your body to keep warm, usually with long sleeves

Reading Part 2

inexpensive (adj) cheap
anniversary (n) (a celebration of) the day an important event happened in a past year
venue (n) place where a public event or meeting happens
romantic (adj) to do with love
atmosphere (n) the feeling or character of a place
serve (v) provide, offer
tournament (n) a sports competition
central (adj) in the centre
location (n) the place where something is
exotic (adj) unusual and often exciting because it comes from a faraway place
delicious (adj) very tasty
book (v) reserve, arrange to have a room, seat or place for a time in the future
budget (n) the amount of money you have available to spend
conveniently (adv) easily available for your needs
luxurious (adj) of high quality and great comfort

decor (n) the colour, style and arrangement of things in a room

reserve (v) book, arrange to have a room, seat or place for a time in the future

outskirts (n pl) areas that are part of a city but outside the city centre

guest (n) someone who is invited to stay or do something in a place

up-to-date (phr) modern, in fashion

affordable (adj) not too expensive, that most people have enough money for

Reading Part 3

personal trainer (n) someone who helps you become fit through an individual programme of exercise

lifeguard (n) someone on a beach or at a swimming pool who keeps people safe and helps them if they are in danger

on duty (prep phr) at work

picnic (n) food and drink which you take to eat outside

competitive (adj) to do with beating someone else

work off (phr v) get rid of

stress (n) feeling of pressure

five-a-side football (n) football with five players on each team

in shape (prep phr) in good physical condition

dieting (n) taking care of what you eat

teamwork (n) working together

balcony (n) an outside area that is above the ground floor of a building

overlook (v) have a view of from above

gardens (n pl) small park with many pretty features

table tennis (n) game played with bats and a small ball and a net on a table, ping pong

darts (n pl) game in which you throw small arrows at a round board to score points

resident (adj) regularly working in a place

make use of (expr) use something

Reading Part 4

tip (n) useful piece of practical advice

run out of (phr v) have less and less of something until you have none

clever (adj) having the ability to learn and understand things quickly and easily

messy (adj) dirty

sooner or later (expr) at some time in the future

at the end of the day (expr) finally, after all

be worth it (expr) have a good result for the amount of time or work used

on the other hand (expr) from a different point of view

concert (n) musical performance

courage (n) bravery, the ability to control fear and deal with danger, pain and uncertainty

publish (v) make available in written form

a good cause (n) charity, organisation or activity to help others

Reading Part 5

background (n) personal history

run (v) manage a business

boarding school (n) school where you live and study

extremely (adv) very

husband (n) man who is married to a woman

research (n) studying and finding out about something

common interest (n) subject you like together with someone else

afterwards (adv) later

bury (v) put something under the ground and cover it

Writing Part 2

promise (v) say for sure that you will do something

Writing Part 3

ring (n) round and usually metal object that you put on your finger

Listening Part 2

membership fee (n) the price you pay to belong to a club or organisation

reduce (v) make less or smaller

discount (n) lower price

Listening Part 3

map (n) plan of a place

leaflet (n) small book with information

tomb (n) large place where somebody is buried

jewellery (n) decorative items that you wear on your body

perfumed (adj) nice-smelling because of using perfumes

oil (n) thick liquid

Speaking Part 3

sightseeing (n) looking at places of interest

Glossary

Practice Test 8

Reading Part 1
Congratulations! (n pl) Well done!
in the end (prep phr) finally
artificial (adj) not natural
flavour (n) taste
in no time (prep phr) very quickly
lift (v) pick up
bent (adj) not straight, bending at the knees
straight (adj) not bent, flat
weight (n) how heavy something is
muscle (n) part of the body that can tighten and relax to produce movement
at a distance (prep phr) not near
lend (v) give something to someone for a period of time expecting it to be given back
give someone a ring (expr) call, telephone someone

Reading Part 2
unplugged (adj) without using microphones or electricity to produce sound
UK (abbr) the United Kingdom (of Great Britain and Northern Ireland)
ballet (n) kind of classical dancing that tells a story or expresses an idea
perform (v) present a show to people
classics (n pl) pieces of music that are well-known and of a high standard and lasting value
stadium (n) large building, often with no roof, that is used for sporting events and concerts
symphony (n) long piece of music for an orchestra
orchestra (n) large group of musicians who play different instruments
classical (adj) music that is part of a long tradition and has lasting value
performance (n) show
stage (n) place where people perform
swan (n) large, usually white bird with a long neck that lives on rivers and lakes
professor (n) well-qualified teacher who usually works at a university
bring alive (phr v) make happen now
masterpiece (n) the greatest work of an artist
band (n) group of musicians
be tired of (phr v) be bored with
cheer somebody up (phr v) make somebody feel happier
fresh (adj) new
guarantee (v) make sure that something happens

join forces (expr) work together
youth club (n) place where young people can meet and do things
influence (v) have an effect on
Kurt Cobain (n) singer and guitarist in the rock group *Nirvana*
Mick Jagger (n) singer in the rock group the *Rolling Stones*
acoustic (adj) not electric music
industry (n) business
decade (n) period of ten years
salsa (n) Latin American style of music and dance
main (adj) most important, biggest
square (n) an open public area
Elvis Presley (n) famous singer and actor
tribute band (n) band that plays songs made famous by another group
It's now or never (expr) if you don't do it now, you won't have the chance again
successor (n) someone who later follows another's style
producer (n) someone who organises things to make a music CD
experimental (adj) trying out new things
album (n) CD with a collection of songs or music

Reading Part 3
village (n) small town
rebuild (v) build again
melt (v) become liquid because of getting hotter
architect (n) someone who designs buildings
designer (n) someone who plans how to make something
gather (v) bring together
sculpt (v) cut stone, wood or other materials to make sculptures
block (n) large piece of hard material, such as stone
accommodation (n) place to stay
cabin (n) small (usually wooden) house
sleeping bag (n) warm bag to sleep in when it's cold
snowmobile (n) vehicle to travel across the snow or ice
sleigh (n) kind of transport on skis usually pulled by animals to travel across ice or snow

Reading Part 4
professional (n) someone who is trained and knows about a subject
perfect (adj) the best

196

stranger (n) someone you don't know
image (n) the way you see or present yourself
make-up (n) colours you put on your face to make you look better
wardrobe (n) collection of clothes
actual (adj) to do with the thing itself
personality (n) the type of person you are, your character
lifestyle (n) the way someone lives
retired (adj) not working because of old age
ordinary (adj) normal, usual
rest (n) what is left of something
top (n) piece of clothing you wear on the top part of your body
couple (n) two
admit (v) say the truth

Reading Part 5
presenter (n) someone who presents a show on TV
camera operator (n) someone who controls the camera in a TV or film studio
department (n) part of an organisation
specialist (n) expert, someone who knows a lot about a particular thing
set up (phr v) organise from the start

script (n) words of a play or film that an actor has to learn
scene (n) part of a film or play
explosion (n) when something like a bomb or car blows up
process (n) series of actions
seem (v) look like, appear to be

Writing Part 1
tidy up (phr v) put things in the right place
dishwasher (n) machine used for washing the dishes
washing machine (n) machine used for washing clothes

Listening Part 2
creative (adj) being able to think of imaginative ideas
material (n) cloth

Listening Part 3
avoid (v) stay away from, try not to use
corner (n) part of the room where two walls meet

Notes

Notes

Notes

Recording Script

Practice Test 1

This is the Preliminary English Test for Schools, Practice Test 1. There are four parts to the test. You will hear each part twice.

Now open your question paper and look at Part One.

PART ONE
There are seven questions in this part. For each question there are three pictures and a short recording. For each question, choose the correct answer, A, B or C.
Before we start, here is an example.
Where did the boy leave his camera?

M: Oh no! I haven't got my camera!
F: But you used it just now to take a photograph of the fountain.
M: Oh, I remember! <u>I put it down on the steps while I was putting my coat on</u>.
F: Well, let's go back quickly – it might still be there.

The answer is A.
Look at the three pictures for question 1 now.

Now we are ready to start. Listen carefully. You will hear each recording twice.

One   What has the boy already eaten today?
M: I can't decide what to order. I had the fish last time and I wasn't very keen on it. Oh, the roast chicken looks nice. I've never tried that here.
F: Why don't you have a nice fresh salad with some tomatoes and lettuce? You like salads, don't you?
M: Yes, <u>but I had salad for lunch at school</u>. I'd prefer something else now, Mum. I know – can I have the roast beef with potatoes? I haven't had beef for ages.

Now listen again.

Two   What does the man want to buy?
F: Have you still got that old motorbike? I thought you'd bought a new one?
M: No, I've still got the same one, but <u>I am thinking of getting a car</u>. I don't like getting wet when it rains all the time. But they're really expensive compared with motorbikes.
F: Well, a bicycle is cheaper, but you'll still get wet!
M: That's true! And it's even slower!

Now listen again.

Three   What does the students' first teacher look like now?
F: I'm sure you won't recognise Mr Grey, our first teacher, when you see him again after all this time. He's changed a lot.
M: Yes, I'm looking forward to seeing him. I remember that he was thin with short blond hair. But that was years ago when we were at primary school.
F: Well, he's very different now. <u>He grew his hair, and now it's quite long.</u> He's still thin, though. Oh, and <u>he's shaved his beard off</u>!

Now listen again.

Four   What is the weather like now?
M: Has it stopped snowing up there yet? You must be very cold.
F: Yes, the temperature is very low. The wind is blowing, but the snow has stopped now, and it's started <u>to rain</u>.

I expect the rain will freeze tonight and in the morning we'll have some frost. I can't wait for the sun to come out again!
M: The forecast says it will be warmer tomorrow, but not in the morning, so stay inside!
F: Don't worry. We've got the central heating on!

Now listen again.

Five   What is the programme about?
Welcome to Shopping Advice, the programme which helps you find the best prices for all types of clothes. This week we'll be looking at where to find the <u>cheapest pair of boots in town</u>. Also, we tell you how to pay less for <u>your next pair of trainers</u>. And if you need anything else, we know where the latest fashion items cost less. First, though, we talk to shoppers in Leeds about what they are buying. Then tune in next week and we'll have some information about coats and gloves for the winter.... [FADE OUT]

Now listen again.

Six   What do they need to buy?
M: Where's the shopping list? I thought I gave it to you. Oh, what are we going to do?
F: I haven't got it. Can you remember what was on it? I think we need milk and lemons, but I can't remember anything else.
M: Oh, here's the list. We don't need milk and <u>it says melons instead of lemons. We need some bread, too</u>.
F: All right. That's over here ...

Now listen again.

Seven   What sport are they talking about?
M: You must be tired after running so much. I certainly am. I don't know how you can do it. And it's so fast! <u>I couldn't even see the ball</u> some of the time!
F: It's OK. It's all about how fit you are. If you're not fit, you can't compete with people who work out at the gym all the time. And of course, you need to know how to play. If <u>you know how to use the racket</u>, and keep running, well, <u>you can win a few points</u>.
M: But not <u>a whole match</u>!

Now listen again.
That is the end of Part One.

PART TWO
Now turn to Part Two, questions 8 to 13. You will hear a teenager named Henry Clark talking about a talent show that he recently took part in. For each question, choose the correct answer A, B or C.
You now have 45 seconds to look at the questions for Part Two.

Now we are ready to start. Listen carefully. You will hear the recording twice.

Being in a talent show wasn't my idea of fun in the beginning. I know I'm a good singer and I feel confident of my abilities. I've been singing for years – since I was a little kid. I sang at my aunt and uncle's wedding when I was eight years old and it was great! I love being in front of crowds. <u>But before the talent show, I'd never competed against anyone. That idea made me nervous.</u>
To be honest, I didn't want to take part in the show. I don't really like competing. I'd rather just sing, you know. I enjoy entertaining people. I want to be a professional singer some day, actually. But <u>my mum said to me, Henry, performers</u>

have to compete with other performers to get singing jobs. A talent show would be a good place to start getting used to that. I realised she was right!

I've taken lots of singing lessons and have had great teachers. I especially liked my teacher, Ms Martha Vine. She encouraged me to do my best. I was sad when she moved away, because I thought I'd never have a teacher as good as her again. But for this talent show, I knew I would need help. I wrote to her and she said she'd come back to help me practise. I was so excited!

We practised for hours. In fact, I sang so much that I developed a problem with my throat. It became very sore, and I had to stop singing for a few days. I was really worried, because the competition was coming up soon. I really didn't want to stop. In the old days, if my throat hurt, I would just give up. But now, things seemed different. I had to be responsible and finish what I had started.

Luckily, a couple of days before the competition, my throat got better. But I had missed hours of practice. Ms Vine told me not to worry. As long as I knew the words to my song, she said, I would be just terrific. I practised a bit more, but the day before the competition, I gave my voice a rest. I wanted to sound my best!

The competition came. I was really quite scared, but I don't know why. I had sung in front of people so many times before. But this time, there would be judges, and other singers. I thought, what if they're all better than me? When it was my turn to sing, I got on stage and, as soon as I opened my mouth, I forgot all about my worries! And I'm so glad I did because I won!

Now listen again.
That is the end of Part Two.

PART THREE
Now turn to Part Three, questions 14 to 19. You will hear some information about a race. For each question, fill in the missing information in the numbered space.
You now have 20 seconds to look at Part Three.

Now we are ready to start. Listen carefully. You will hear the recording twice.

Now, for those of our students who are interested in sport, here's a great opportunity to get some exercise and do something for the school community too.

Our school fun run is on at the end of the month, on the twenty-sixth of April. Here are the details. The race will begin at half past ten. All runners, please meet at the starting point by ten o'clock.

As you all know, our school fun run has taken place every year for thirty years now. Ted Mandrake, one of the school's most famous ex-students, first started the tradition with a two-kilometre run. The fun run became a longer six-kilometre race just five years ago. As always, a few adults who used to be students of the school will also be allowed to take part. They have all become well-known celebrities.

So, here's your opportunity to run a race against celebrities and be photographed with them. And what's more, you'll be able to raise money for this year's project. This year we're trying to raise money to buy more e-readers for our digital library.

So, if you want to have fun and help our school, all you need is a pair of trainers, your tracksuit – and a smile! And if you're afraid that you can't run the whole six kilometres, don't worry – there are shorter races of four kilometres and two kilometres. Also, if you want to run with your little brother or sister or your pet, there are special races for you too! Finally, you won't be running for nothing! The first prize is a brand new bicycle, and those who come second and third will get a pair of roller skates each. And don't be disappointed if you don't win. Everybody who takes part in the race will get a T-shirt as a souvenir. Sign up now!

Now listen again.
That is the end of Part Three.

PART FOUR
Now turn to Part Four, questions 20 to 25. Look at the six sentences for this part. You will hear a conversation between a girl, Carla, and a boy, Jason, where they give their opinions on wearing school uniforms. Decide if each sentence is correct or incorrect. If it is correct, choose the letter A for YES. If it is not correct, choose the letter B for NO.
You now have twenty seconds to look at the questions for Part Four.

Now we are ready to start. Listen carefully. You will hear the recording twice.

F: Hey, Jason, I haven't seen you for a very long time. What have you been doing?
M: Hello Carla, it's nice to see you again. I've been busy. I've got a weekend job in the sandwich bar near my house so I haven't been here for months. Is that your new school uniform?
F: Yes it is. I moved house and changed schools last term! Haven't we met since then? I thought you knew.
M: No, I didn't! So you have to wear a uniform now? That must be awful!
F: Mmm … I'm not sure. It's actually OK. It's not such a bad thing, you know.
M: But don't you want to choose your own clothes?
F: Yes, but on the other hand, I don't have to think about what I want to wear every morning – it's all ready for me! Do you see what I mean?
M: OK. You've got a point there. But I really wouldn't want to wear a uniform. I'd hate to look exactly like everybody else. I want to stand out!
F: I know you do, but what about the kids who stand out because they can't afford nice clothes? One good thing about uniforms is that everyone wears exactly the same clothes. You can't tell who's got rich parents and who hasn't. Don't you think that's a good idea?
M: That's true actually. I hadn't thought of that. Some kids at my school get teased because of what they wear. Uniforms would stop that.
F: That's right! So you see, I don't mind wearing it. I think it's a good thing, but I admit that I do miss wearing my own clothes at school sometimes, too.
M: Yes, I'm sure you do, but look on the bright side! You don't need so many other clothes anymore. You can wear whatever you like in the evenings and weekends and things won't wear out so fast. You're absolutely right! School uniforms aren't such terrible things after all!

Now listen again.
That is the end of the test.

Practice Test 2

This is the Preliminary English Test for Schools, Practice Test 2. There are four parts to the test. You will hear each part twice.

Now open your question paper and look at Part One.

PART ONE
There are seven questions in this part. For each question, there are three pictures and a short recording. For each question, choose the correct answer A, B or C.
Before we start, here is an example.
What does the girl buy?

M: Hello, can I help you?
F: Yes, I'm looking for a new pair of shoes. Well, boots really. I only brought sandals with me on holiday, but I need something stronger to go on the walking tours.
M: Well, we have these black boots, which are very comfortable.

F: What about those over there? <u>I'd prefer light-coloured ones</u>.
M: If you like those, you're in luck because they're in the sale.
F: Great, <u>I'll take them</u>!

The answer is A.
Look at the three pictures for question 1 now.

Now we are ready to start. Listen carefully. You will hear each recording twice.

One   What is Jenny doing on Saturday?
F1:   Have you got any plans for Saturday, Sally?
F2:   Well, I was supposed to go shopping with Jenny, but <u>she has to look after her brother</u> now.
F1:   Oh, that's a shame. Why don't you call Penny and see if she's free? You could invite her round to watch a film.
F2:   Yeah, that's a good idea!
F1:   Just don't forget that we're visiting Grandpa in the evening, so tell her to come at about lunchtime.

Now listen again.

Two   Which film did Emma want to see?
M1:   How was the cinema?
M2:   A bit disappointing really. I wanted to see the new comedy, but it was sold out. Then, Emma and I couldn't decide whether to watch the horror or the romantic film. Of course, Emma didn't want to see the horror film!
M1:   So what did you see in the end?
M2:   <u>The romance, like Emma wanted from the start</u>. It was awful!

Now listen again.

Three What will listeners hear first on the radio show?
Welcome to Friday night on Radio FM. This is Bob Jones and tonight we have a very special show. We'll be interviewing our mystery pop star at eight o'clock and at nine we'll be talking about this week's top films to see at the cinema. <u>Before all that, though, we'll be playing all the best music,</u> starting right now!

Now listen again.

Four   What new item of clothing is the boy wearing?
F: Is that a new jacket?
M: No, I've had it for ages. I did actually buy a new coat yesterday, but I took it back because the zip was broken.
F: Oh, did you get a different one instead, then?
M: Well, no. I didn't see another one I liked so I spent the money on <u>these new jeans</u>. Do you like them?
F: Yeah, they're nice, but I would have bought a coat if I were you. It's going to snow tomorrow!

Now listen again.

Five   Where is the girl going on holiday?
M: How was the school skiing trip?
F: I couldn't go! I twisted my ankle the week before and couldn't even walk on it.
M: What a shame!
F: Yeah, I was really disappointed, but maybe I'll get the chance to go on a skiing holiday next year. Actually, my parents felt so sorry for me that they booked a <u>beach holiday</u> for us all to go on this summer!
M: Wow, that's amazing. I'm going to London in June, but I wish I was going somewhere hot!

Now listen again.

Six   Where did Nick find the wallet?
M1:   Nick, it's six o'clock! Where have you been?

M2:   At the police station. I found a wallet on my way home from school so I took it there.
M1:   Oh, where was it?
M2:   On the pavement <u>outside the post office</u>. There was no one around so I didn't want to leave it there.
M1:   You did the right thing.

Now listen again.

Seven What are they going to do?
F: I'm bored!
M: Haven't you got any homework to do?
F: Yes, I have. But I'm not really in the mood to do homework.
M: Do you want to <u>watch a DVD</u>, then? I've got a great one called War Horse.
F: Oh, I've read the book! My mum gave it to me. It's really good.
M: So, do you want to watch it?
F: Yeah, <u>put it on</u>. It should be interesting.

Now listen again.
That is the end of Part One.

PART TWO
Now turn to Part Two, questions 8 to 13. You will hear an announcement about a new documentary. For each question, choose the correct answer A, B or C.
You now have 45 seconds to look at the questions for Part Two.

Now we are ready to start. Listen carefully. You will hear the recording twice.

For students and anyone else who loves programmes full of <u>information and general knowledge</u>, you're in for a treat tonight. A new documentary is starting on Channel Two at eight o'clock.
Channel Two has brought us plenty of documentaries over the past year, including the popular People and Places, about people and tribes in countries all over the world. Tonight's documentary, however, is a little different. It is the first in a series of documentaries, called Our Planet, about <u>the natural world</u>. The series, which will be shown over eight weeks, will cover topics like hills and mountains, deserts and plains, seas and oceans and, of course, stars and space.
The series will be presented by Professor Joan Mason, <u>an expert in natural sciences</u> and a teacher at one of the UK's top universities. She'll take you through each unique landscape to talk about how they formed and what effects they have on our planet, as well as giving you plenty of amazing information and facts.
Each documentary will also have special guests, depending on the topic. These experts <u>will explain our amazing planet in a simple and straightforward way</u>, so the programmes will be easy to understand for anyone over ten years old. Tonight some of the world's top astronomers will talk about stars.
If that isn't impressive enough, the new technology used to make tonight's documentary means that you'll be taken on a journey through space to the stars! With the help of pictures sent from <u>cameras, satellites and computers,</u> you can now see exactly what space is really like. Tonight you'll learn <u>how stars are born, what happens to a star when it dies</u> and how scientists think planet Earth was formed.
Don't forget to switch on tonight, and every Tuesday night at eight, to catch this incredible documentary.

Now listen again.
That is the end of Part Two.

PART THREE
Now turn to Part Three, questions 14 to 19. You will hear a man giving a walking tour of a castle. For each question, fill in the missing information in the numbered space.
You now have 20 seconds to look at Part Three.

Now we are ready to start. Listen carefully. You will hear the recording twice.

Welcome to Powderham Castle, one of the most beautiful castles in Devon. I think you're really going to enjoy your school trip today! Our walking tour includes a tour of the castle rooms as well as the rose garden. The tour will last about one hour, and afterwards refreshments will be served in the dining hall. If you'd like to take pictures at any point, please do so. Now, if everyone's ready, let's begin!
Our first room is the castle library. This library contains hundreds of antique books, some of which are several centuries old. They are well looked after and many of them haven't been read in over a hundred years. I have to ask you not to touch any of them so that they can stay here for another few centuries. Members of the Courtenay family would sit in this room and read by the fireplace which is how many people spent their evenings before the invention of television.
Our next room is the dining room. This is where many famous friends of the Courtenay family enjoyed meals prepared by the region's best chefs. The dining room has seating for over one hundred guests. Also on display are the plates and silverware that the family used over the years. The next room we visit before we step outside is the kitchen. Here you can see what life would have been like for the kitchen staff in the 1800s. Imagine, many of the servants were in their teens, like yourselves. The kitchen has got large wooden tables for preparing food. There is also a large selection of knives for cutting meat, as it was common to eat meat with every meal.
Just outside, we have the walled rose garden. It leads to a wooded area and a park with deer in the castle grounds. Near the deer park is a small version of the castle, where our younger visitors enjoy playing after the tour.
We end our tour in the Courtenay Gallery. Here we have a display of royal robes and other items worn by the late Earl of Devon. There's also a short documentary on the history of the castle. Feel free to spend as much time as you like in the castle grounds. I hope you enjoyed the tour. Now does anyone have any questions?

Now listen again.
That is the end of Part Three.

PART FOUR
Now turn to Part Four, questions 20 to 25. Look at the six sentences for this part. You will hear a conversation between a girl, Olivia, and a boy, Joe, about exams and tests. Decide if each sentence is correct or incorrect. If it is correct, choose the letter A for YES. If it is not correct, choose the letter B for NO. You now have 20 seconds to look at the questions for Part Four.

Now we are ready to start. Listen carefully. You will hear the recording twice.

F: Are you ready for the test on Monday, Joe?
M: I guess so. I've read through all my class notes and last week's homework. And I passed last week's test, so I'm sure I'll do well.
F: Yeah, what more can you do? I'm pretty prepared too, but I don't really see the point in having a little test every week. It seems a bit silly to me, and to be honest, I'd rather just study for one big exam at the end of term.
M: Really? Not me! I think it's better if you do a little bit of studying more often. Okay, so we have to revise and do a test every week, but when the big exam comes, we'll remember most of the things because we've been doing revision all through the year.
F: Maybe you're right. There's always loads to do and learn for exams, so breaking it down into sections and small tests makes sense. I just find that I get stressed out every week about these little tests, especially because we normally have so much homework to do

as well. At least when we have exams, they're the only thing we have to focus on.
M: You have a point. I guess in the end it depends on what the teachers and the school prefer.
F: What do you mean?
M: Well, if students do better in the exams when they have tests all through the year, then they'll keep giving us tests.
F: Yeah, it definitely makes the school look good if all the students get good marks. It would be interesting to see how many students agree, though. I mean how many prefer to do tests every week and how many would rather just do one big exam at the end of the year?
M: I think most people would say the tests help in the end. I know I definitely would!

Now listen again.
That is the end of the test.

Practice Test 3

This is the Preliminary English Test for Schools, Practice Test 3. There are four parts to the test. You will hear each part twice.

Now open your question paper and look at Part One.

PART ONE
There are seven questions in this part. For each question there are three pictures and a short recording. For each question, choose the correct answer (A, B or C).
Before we start, here is an example.
Where does the boy want to go?

M: Excuse me, I think I'm a bit lost. They told me to follow the signs for the swimming pool, but I can't see any signs and …
F: Where do you want to go?
M: To my friend's house. It's near the underground station, right next to the swimming pool.
F: Oh, that's easy. Go left at the next street and then go straight along Green Street, and you'll find the swimming pool on your left-hand side.
M: Thank you.

The answer is B.
Look at the three pictures for question 1 now.

Now we are ready to start. Listen carefully. You will hear each recording twice.

One   What time does the next bus pass?
F: Oh no! I told you we should have left ten minutes ago. Now we've missed the ten past five bus! Oh, my mother is going to be furious with me now! It's all your fault!
M: Calm down, calm down. It's not so bad. There's another bus in five minutes, at quarter past. Look at the timetable.
F: No, that's the timetable for weekdays and today is Saturday. The next bus is in twenty minutes, at half past five. Oh, what shall I do?
M: Here, why don't you use my mobile to call your mum? I'm sure she'll understand.
F: Oh, OK. Thanks.

Now listen again.

Two   When was the last time the woman had her earrings on?
M: OK, Mum, do you remember the last time you were wearing them? I mean was it at work or was it at that party last Saturday? When was it?
F: I definitely had them on at work on Friday, I remember that. And then I changed clothes and I took them off

and left them on the bedside table, next to the rest of my jewellery. Then, <u>on Saturday, when your dad and I went to my boss's party, I put on the earrings</u>, together with the bracelet you gave me and the necklace – they go so well together!

M: Yes, I know, I really like them together. So what happened next?

F: <u>While we were there, the earrings started hurting me a bit, so I gave them to Dad to put in his pocket. That was the last time I saw them.</u>

Now listen again.

Three What is Peter's hobby?

F: Hey, Peter! What's up? I haven't seen you for ages!

M: Hi, Melanie. Yes, I've been very busy recently. I've been preparing for the race.

F: Oh? What race? Are you taking part in the marathon next week?

M: What? Me? You know me, I hate running! I'm not the sporty type – not in the slightest!

F: So what race is it?

M: You know next week is the big swimming race, right? <u>Well, after that there's going to be a race between model boats made by students. That's what I'm taking part in!</u> I've made one and I'm going to race it! Would you like to come and see? It's going to be great fun!

F: Sure, what time?

Now listen again.

Four How will the father and son spend their day tomorrow?

M1: So, what are we going to do tomorrow? Have you thought about it at all?

M2: Well, I thought perhaps we could go to the funfair. It's good fun!

M1: Hmm, we've done that so many times. I'd like something different this time. How about going to the zoo instead?

M2: Oh, Dad! I'm not ten! I've been to the zoo a million times. It's boring! Besides, what will my friends think? They'll laugh!

M1: <u>How about going cycling in the forest, then? We can have a picnic and you can invite some of your friends along, too.</u>

M2: <u>Great! Let's do that!</u> I'll call Adrian and Callum.

Now listen again.

Five What does the teacher tell the children to bring with them?

Now, remember that tomorrow we are visiting the National Park in the Brecon Beacons. So don't forget to wear warm clothes and <u>bring a waterproof jacket with you.</u> Also, you need to wear waterproof walking boots and have some extra warm clothes just in case you get wet. Don't forget to bring a packed lunch and a water bottle with you as there is no restaurant or canteen there. Finally, please don't take valuable electronic equipment with you as we don't want anything to get lost or broken. Oh, and please remember that mobile phones don't have a signal in the park, so you won't be able to use them during the day. See you tomorrow morning! Be on time!

Now listen again.

Six Which film are they going to watch?

M: Look, Mum! Can we rent this DVD? It's about hip-hop musicians. It'll be great!

F: Come on, Sam, you know I don't like hip-hop much, and nor does your dad. We need to rent a film that all the family can enjoy. How about this one – Space Walker? It's a science-fiction film.

M: What? No way! It doesn't sound very exciting and you know that neither Dad nor I like science fiction. <u>What about an action film?</u>

F: Oh, OK. I guess we can all enjoy something like that. <u>Shall we get the latest James Bond film, then?</u>

Now listen again.

Seven What is Nick going to do next?

F: Hi, Nick. You don't look very well. What's the matter?

M: I've got a maths test next week and I haven't studied enough and I'm too tired and I can't think and I'm …

F: Relax! Take it easy. There's plenty of time. A break will do you good. Why don't you go for a short walk? It'll help your brain work better.

M: No, I don't have time! <u>I have to pick up my little sister from nursery school.</u> I promised Mum I'd help her today.

F: Well, that's a walk, too, you know, and a break from studying!

M: So it is, I suppose. See you tomorrow at school. Bye!

Now listen again.
That is the end of Part One.

PART TWO

Now turn to Part Two, questions 8 to 13. You will hear part of an interview with a boy called Arthur Hobbs, who started a company which makes candles. For each question, choose the correct answer A, B or C.
You now have 45 seconds to look at the questions for Part 2.

Now we are ready to start. Listen carefully. You will hear the recording twice.

F: Today, we have Arthur Hobbs with us, a very young, but very successful businessman. Welcome, Arthur. So, tell us how you got this idea for your business.

M: It started as a joke really. My school teacher suggested that our class could sell some candles she'd made to raise money for a charity. But I told her that boys wouldn't buy them because all her candles had smells for girls!

F: Smells for girls? What do you mean?

M: Well, they had sweet, flowery smells – stuff that girls like, really. Then I <u>thought it would be cool if there were candles with scents that boys liked to smell.</u>

F: Oh? What smells do boys like?

M: I thought of how the grass smells on our football pitch, for example. My teacher didn't think that I could make anything out of that idea at first.

F: So what happened?

M: I talked about the idea with my football team mates. They agreed it would be fun to try and maybe we could also raise money for our club. We had a club meeting with our parents and they all agreed to help. Each team member's family paid thirty euros. I added fifty euros that I'd saved up, so that was enough to get started. <u>But I had to promise them that if my business plan didn't work out, I'd pay the team back from my pocket money.</u>

F: I'm sure <u>that made you a bit anxious, didn't it?</u>

M: <u>Yes,</u> but it also motivated me to work hard and be serious about the project, you know. If you risk losing your money, then you're very careful and you work very hard. I <u>also wanted to earn some money for a new bike</u> as my parents couldn't afford it, so I really wanted the project to succeed.

F: So that's how you started. Did you have any help making the candles?

M: I certainly did – the whole team helped. And here's the interesting part, the candle business helps the environment, too! <u>I think it's great when you can find a useful way to recycle things!</u> We had the great idea to use food cans. First, we asked our classmates to bring empty cans to school. Now we collect them once a week. Then we clean the cans well and dry them. After that, we fill them with candle wax in different scents – you know – smells like grass or leather. When they're ready, we take them to the shops and sell them.

F: Was it easy to find customers? I mean, did shops want to sell your candles at first? The scents are a bit unusual.

M: It wasn't easy at first, but some shops agreed to sell them and then more and more people showed an interest in them. Now we also sell them online. I got my dream bike and we've raised enough money to paint the club house!

F: So what are your plans for the future? Will you keep making candles?

M: I think it's been a very interesting experience and I've learnt a lot from it. It definitely is very hard work to have a business. Next year, I'll have to focus more on studying for exams at school, so I probably won't have time for making more candles, but I'll always remember what I've learnt from this and maybe I'll try to start a business like that again one day.

F: Well, that's an amazing success story. Thank you for coming here to share it with our listeners, Arthur. And good luck! And now to … [FADE OUT]

Now listen again.
That is the end of Part Two.

PART THREE

Now turn to Part Three, questions 14 to 19. You will hear some information about a book. For each question, fill in the missing information in the numbered space.
You now have 20 seconds to look at Part 3.

Now we are ready to start. Listen carefully. You will hear the recording twice.

Now, next on our list is the book of the week! All of you who love a good story will, I'm sure, enjoy this week's suggestion. It's a book by Michael Ende – let me spell that for you if you want to ask for the book: E - N - D - E. This famous German author wrote books that have entertained generations of children and teenagers throughout the world. He wrote the book in German in 1979 and then it was translated into English in 1983.
The Neverending Story is the adventure of a very unhappy teenage boy , Bastian. His mother has died and his father hasn't spent much time with him since then. Bastian also feels lonely because he hasn't got many school friends and some of the boys at his school are cruel to him. Then one day something happens that changes his life. While he is trying to get away from some boys from his school, Bastian runs into an antique bookshop. There, he picks up a strange book. He can't put the book down, so he steals it from the shop and runs away. In a small room in the school, he begins to read the strange book. This is where things start to get really weird! While he's reading, he suddenly becomes a part of the story.
In the story, Bastian meets a boy called Atreyu, who is trying to save the magic world in the book. The name of this world is Fantastica. Together the boys try to solve the mystery of what is slowly destroying Fantastica. However, while they are having lots of adventures together, something terrible happens to Bastian. He slowly begins losing his memory, until he can't remember who he is anymore. Then his new friend Atreyu helps him find a way to remember things. In the end, they also help Bastian's father, who has got lost, too.
The book is full of action and mystery. Some parts of the story may be a bit too scary for young children, but anyone over twelve years old is sure to love it. So if you like a good adventure story about magic, monsters, dragons and heroes, then you'll definitely enjoy reading The Neverending Story!

Now listen again.
That is the end of Part Three.

PART FOUR

Now turn to Part Four, questions 20 to 25. Look at the six sentences for this part. You will hear a conversation between a boy, Stuart, and a girl, Erica, about a television programme called 'Kids Can Cook', a reality cooking show which teenagers take part in. Decide if each sentence is correct or incorrect. If it is correct, choose the letter A for YES. If it is not correct, choose the letter B for NO.
You now have 20 seconds to look at the questions for Part Four.

Now we are ready to start. Listen carefully. You will hear the recording twice.

F: So, Stuart, did you see Kids Can Cook last night?

M: Well, I missed the first part of it because I had to meet with my team mates for football practice and I didn't get home in time, but I saw most of it. It was an exciting episode, don't you think?

F: Yeah, it was great! All the kids were really nervous because they had to cook a meal for a famous person and they didn't know who they were cooking for. All they knew was that the person didn't like beef and wasn't keen on vegetables, except tomatoes.

M: Yeah, that was a bit of a challenge. My favourite dish was the fish burger. That was really interesting, wasn't it? It looked very tasty and also quite healthy, and the only vegetables were lettuce and tomato. I was sure that dish was going to win.

F: Well, I'm not crazy about fish, but I agree that it looked healthy. My favourite was the chicken and rice with lemon sauce. It looked really delicious. I wish I could make something like that. It's nice that they show the recipes on TV. Although I'm not very good at cooking.

M: My mum says practice makes perfect when it comes to cooking. She's made a few things that weren't so nice the first time round, but sometimes she makes them again and they're better. The only thing I know how to make is pizza.

F: Oh, that's not easy to make, actually. You have to be very talented in the kitchen. How do you make the pizza dough?

M: Well, the first thing I do is I turn the oven on to 200 degrees Celsius and wait a few minutes for it to get warm. Then I take the pizza out of the freezer, take it out of the box, take off the plastic, and put it in the oven. It's ready in 15 minutes!

F: Um, wait a second, Stuart. Are you telling me all you can do is cook a frozen pizza? There's no talent there! Even my little sister could do that!

M: Well, it's easy to burn a pizza in the oven. I'm talented enough to know when to take it out.

F: Right, when the oven goes DING!

Now listen again.
That is the end of the test.

Practice Test 4

This is the Preliminary English Test for Schools, Practice Test 4. There are four parts to the test. You will hear each part twice.

Now open your question paper and look at Part One.

PART ONE

There are seven questions in this part. For each question there are three pictures and a short recording. For each question, choose the correct answer (A, B or C).
Before we start, here is an example.
What time are the boys meeting?

M1: Hey, Mike. What time is the film on tonight?
M2: I think it starts at quarter past eight. But we should get there half an hour earlier to get the tickets.
M1: OK. So shall we meet at quarter to eight?
M2: Erm ... Let's say seven thirty. Then we'll have time to buy some popcorn too.
M1: OK. See you then!

The answer is A.
Look at the three pictures for question 1 now.

Now we are ready to start. Listen carefully. You will hear each recording twice.

One   How is the girl getting to school?
F: Could you drive me to school today, Dad?
M: Sorry, Tina. I haven't got the car. Your mum's taken it. You'll have to take the bus today.
F: You know I hate taking the bus, Dad. It takes ages and it costs too much! I'd rather go by bike.
M: Don't be silly! It's freezing cold outside! Here's some money. Now, run or you'll miss it!
F: Well, maybe you're right. It is cold today. Thanks, Dad. See you later!

Now listen again.

Two   What did the girl forget?
M: Can we use your laptop to work on our history project? I've left mine at home.
F: OK, no problem. We have to hand it in next week, so we'd better get started. But have you got a CD to save the project on when we've finished?
M: Yes. I've got two in my bag. I don't use CDs much these days, but that's what the teacher wants. Good thing I remembered to bring them!
F: Great! Before we start, can I use your mobile to call my mum and let her know we're at the library? I left mine charging at home and forgot to bring it with me.
M: No problem. Here you are.
F: Thanks, Jake. You're a star.

Now listen again.

Three What was the final score?
The Spanish team lost to United last Saturday after a long and exciting match. Rodriguez scored the only two goals in the first half, putting the home team way ahead; a disappointing score for the 4,000 United fans who had travelled to Spain to watch their team. The Barcelona players tried hard to score again in the second half, but they were out of luck. United scored three spectacular goals in the last ten minutes! United fans went crazy at their two – three victory. What a match!

Now listen again.

Four   What are they going to play?
F1: I see you've brought your rackets, Tracy. Do you fancy playing tennis? I'm tired of sunbathing!
F2: Me too! I wouldn't mind a game, but I can't find the ball.
F1: That's a pity. How about playing cards? My mum taught me a new game the other day! It's quite easy.
F2: Cards? No thanks. Can we play that new game you have on your phone? The one you downloaded.
F1: OK. Oh no! We can't! I forgot to charge it. Sorry! So I'll teach you to play Mum's card game. You'll like it. I promise!

Now listen again.

Five   Where will the boy do the English course?
M: Mrs Johnson, I'm going to do an English course this summer in the UK. Do you think I should go to London, Edinburgh or Oxford? I've heard about courses in all of them.

F: Hmm. That's a difficult choice. London's such a huge city and it's always busy. Edinburgh's smaller than London and I think people there are very friendly. But it might be a bit cold for you, so what about Oxford?
M: Well, I've already been to Oxford. And I'm not keen on cooler weather. Also, I'd really like to go to all the museums in London. The course lasts four weeks, so maybe I could visit Oxford and Edinburgh at the weekends.
F: Well, that's a long way to travel for a weekend. But it sounds like you've made your decision. I hope you get a place on the course.

Now listen again.

Six   What does the boy need help with?
M: Mum, can you help me? I was showing the photos we took in Paris to Grandpa and now my computer is stuck.
F: Why don't you ask your brother? I don't want to do something and make things worse.
M: He's already tried to help me but he couldn't fix it. Please, Mum.
F: OK. Let me have a look. There we go. That's sorted. You should be able to open the files again now.
M: Thanks, Mum! Don't turn it off. I'm going to help Grandpa choose a photo to print!

Now listen again.

Seven What is the girl going to wear to the party?
M: Where are you going, Sissy?
F: To Betty's party. It was her birthday on Monday. What do you think of this dress? Does it look too formal? I was going to wear that skirt I bought last week, but it's in the washing machine.
M: What about your black trousers?
F: I've been wearing them for two days. I can't wear the same thing again.
M: Well, then, you look fine as you are! Have fun!
F: Thanks, Michael. You're the best brother in the world.

Now listen again.
That is the end of Part One.

PART TWO
Now turn to Part Two, questions 8 to 13. You will hear a school reporter interviewing Paul Reynolds, a journalist, who wrote an article on unusual or dangerous jobs. For each question, choose the correct answer A, B or C.
You now have 45 seconds to look at the questions for Part 2.

Now we are ready to start. Listen carefully. You will hear the recording twice.

F: Paul Reynolds, journalist for News Today, is here to tell us about his most recent article, Strange Jobs. Hello, Paul.
M: Hi!
F: The first unusual job you mention in your article is a greetings card writer. What do these writers actually do?
M: Well, they write the message that we see either on the front of greetings cards or on the inside. Some writers are also designers, so they also design the card or even draw the picture on it.
F: How interesting! Is it a difficult job?
M: There aren't many words on most cards, so people think they're easy to write. The truth is that it's quite complicated. These days, people like to send greetings cards for a huge range of reasons. The most popular are for birthdays and other celebrations. Then there are different kinds of well-wishing cards, for example to send to people who are ill, or even taking an exam. The writer has to think of a wish that is original, but also something that most people would say. The card

207

shouldn't have too many words; it should be clear and funny – if it's a funny card, of course.

F: I see. And how much does a greetings card writer get paid?

M: With each verse or wish, the writer could earn from ten to five hundred euros. Card writers don't get very rich, but the money isn't bad if you think it's just a couple of lines.

F: Not at all! And what about the next job – the window cleaner?

M: Ah, yes! Did you know that this is the most dangerous job?

F: Why's that, Paul?

M: Because those who do this job sometimes wash windows of very tall buildings. Imagine the window cleaners in big city centres. They have to clean all the high buildings – even the tallest skyscrapers! Of course, they have protection and they don't work if it's too windy or if it's raining.

F: So, can anyone become a window cleaner if they want to?

M: No, you have to be quite strong because it's a tiring, physical job. You don't have to be tall, but you need to be good at climbing. So you mustn't be afraid of heights!

F: Of course! Do window cleaners usually work long hours?

M: Yes, most window cleaners start early in the morning and work until the late afternoon. They need light to see what they're doing and to clean the windows properly, so they stop when it gets dark.

F: Thank you very much, Paul.

M: My pleasure!

Now listen again.
That is the end of Part Two.

PART THREE

Now turn to Part Three, questions 14 to 19. You will hear a weather report on the radio. For each question, fill in the missing information in the numbered space.
You now have 20 seconds to look at Part 3.

Now we are ready to start. Listen carefully. You will hear the recording twice.

Hi there! Next on Teen Radio, let's have a quick look at the weather. This week so far has been very warm, but from tomorrow, Thursday, I'm afraid this is going to change. It's going to get a lot more cloudy on Thursday morning, and that cloud's going to remain throughout the day. You can forget about the lovely days we've been having as temperatures are going to drop by six to ten degrees! In the north, it's going to stay below twelve degrees during the day, whereas in the south it'll be a little bit warmer. Particularly in the south-west, temperatures could reach fifteen degrees at midday, with Thursday night being a bit cooler, around thirteen degrees. From the early hours of Friday morning, there's going to be heavy rain over much of the country. However, it'll have dried up by the evening, but it'll still be quite cold. So don't forget to take a jacket with you if you're going out anywhere.
Now let's see how the weekend looks. It's certainly going to be a few degrees warmer and brighter. Saturday will be a sunny spring day with hardly any clouds, but Sunday won't be quite as pleasant. It's not going to rain – we can expect another sunny day with temperatures a little higher than average for April, but strong winds will be blowing from the north. If you're thinking about going for a bike ride on Sunday, be extremely careful; road conditions could be dangerous because of this. It'll be a great day for windsurfing though! Whatever you do, take care and have a great time!

Now listen again.
That is the end of Part Three.

PART FOUR

Now turn to Part Four, questions 20 to 25. Look at the six sentences for this part. You will hear a conversation between a girl, Rebecca, and a boy, Steve, who live in a small town. Decide if each sentence is correct or incorrect. If it is correct, choose the letter A for YES. If it is not correct, choose the letter B for NO.
You now have twenty seconds to look at the questions for Part 4.

Now we are ready to start. Listen carefully. You will hear the recording twice.

F: How was your weekend, Steve? Did you go out at all?

M: I was going to. I'd planned to go to the cinema to watch Scary City, but …

F: What cinema? They've just closed the only cinema in Amersham!

M: I know, silly! My mum was going to drive me into London, but we had to change our plans at the last minute. Granddad wasn't feeling well, so Mum had to get the doctor to come and see him. Luckily, it was nothing serious. After that, it was too late to go to the cinema and I just stayed at home and played Wizards and Dragons on the computer with Patrick.

F: Not again! Aren't you tired of playing that game? It's so boring and really old! My sister has just bought a new one. I think it's called Fantastic Five. We've only played it once, but it's not bad.

M: Yes, I've heard it's quite good – I hope she'll let me play it some time.

F: I'm sure she will, next time you come round here. Anyway, are you doing anything tomorrow morning? We've got the day off school, so let's get out and enjoy it.

M: I don't know. There's not much to do in this place. I wish Amersham had a better sports centre. It'd be great if we had a modern gym or even an indoor basketball court … but we don't of course.

F: Yes, I know what you mean. But there are still lots of things we can do outdoors. We're lucky that way. Hey! Let's go cycling tomorrow and have a picnic in the park – if it's not raining, of course.

M: That's a great idea, Rebecca! But it'll have to be after eleven o'clock. I've got to finish my geography homework and take some books back to the library. Can you bring your camera? I'm afraid mine's broken.

F: OK, I'll bring mine. Shall we say half past eleven, at the school?

M: Half past eleven sounds perfect. But maybe it's better to meet in front of the museum because we won't have so many busy roads to cross. Then we can ride straight into the park and have lunch there.

F: Great! I'll see you there.

Now listen again.
That is the end of the test.

Practice Test 5

This is the Preliminary English Test for Schools, Practice Test 5. There are four parts to the test. You will hear each part twice.

Now open your question paper and look at Part One.

PART ONE

There are seven questions in this part. For each question there are three pictures and a short recording. For each question, choose the correct answer (A, B or C).
Before we start, here is an example.
What job does the boy want to do?

F: Do you know what you want to be when you grow up, Mark?

M: Not really. I mean, a lot of kids say they want to be doctors because it's a well-paid job, but I think it's really hard. What about you, Linda?
F: I want to do what my uncle does. He's a cameraman in a film studio. I think that's an interesting job because he works with different people and films different types of scenes every day.
M: That's great. My mum's a chef, and I've always liked cooking, so maybe I'll give that a try.

The answer is C.
Look at the three pictures for question 1 now.

Now we are ready to start. Listen carefully. You will hear each recording twice.

One   What did Dennis leave at school?
F: Dennis, where are you?
M: I'm downstairs, Mum. I'm getting ready to go out to meet Brian and Paul for pizza.
F: OK. Well, it looks like it's going to rain. Have you got your raincoat on?
M: No, but I'm wearing my jacket. I think I left my raincoat at school yesterday. Oh, wait a second! Here it is, in the wardrobe.
F: Oh, good. Don't forget your umbrella, either.
M: Umbrella? Oops! It's not here. Looks like I left that in the classroom.

Now listen again.

Two   What is the boy having a problem with?
M: Hey Pauline, can you take a look at my computer? I'm having a problem with it.
F: OK, what's up?
M: Well, I can't get my mouse to work. Look – when I move it, nothing happens on the screen. I can't understand it. Do you think I need a new one?
F: Maybe not. Let's see. OK, it's plugged in to the computer, so that's not the problem. Just a moment, let me see your keyboard. There you go. How about that?
M: Wow! It's working again. I still don't know what happened, but thanks for fixing it, Sis!

Now listen again.

Three   Where is the man going first?
Hi, Sarah. I'm just calling to say that I'm going to be a little late getting home. I'm still going to the supermarket to pick up something for dinner, just like we talked about. But before that I've got to go to the post office to send this parcel today, so it'll arrive on time. I've also got to return to the university for a meeting later this evening. Of course, I'll do that after dinner, or else I'll be starving. OK, that's all for now, see you soon!

Now listen again.

Four   What did Irene injure the most?
M: I heard you've had an accident, Irene. Are you OK?
F: I'm getting better now, thanks, Uncle Mike. . But the left side of my body is still sore. The doctor gave me a prescription for the pain. I won't be able to walk very well for a while.
M: Oh, no, that's awful. I didn't realise it was so serious.
F: Yes, it is. I broke my ankle, so it will be a while before it's better. My shoulder hurts a bit and my knee is sore too, but it's just got a cut on it.

Now listen again.

Five   What's the last programme about?
Good evening, listeners. Tonight on Radio Seven, we've got your favourite nature documentary, Outdoor Life, where world-famous explorer Bill Singer is taking us on a trip through Camden Forest, to tell us about the area as we listen to forest sounds. Then it's Music Hour with Jim Stephens, who's interviewing world-famous guitar player, Jackie Smith. But first, we've got Quick Trip with Joan Paulsen, who's got a special on car ferries in northern Europe. So stay with us for an interesting evening … [FADE OUT]

Now listen again.

Six   What does the girl order?
M1: What would you like to order?
M2: I'd like a chicken sandwich with mustard, tomato and lettuce, please. And a mineral water.
M1: OK. And for you, Miss?
F: I think I'll have a large slice of pizza.
M1: Oh, I'm sorry. We're out of pizza at the moment. Is there something else you'd like to have?
F: Hmm, let me see. Perhaps I'll have a salad. Do you have spinach salad?
M1: Yes, we do. And it's freshly made, of course.
F: OK. I'll have that, please.

Now listen again.

Seven   What sport does the girl want to do?
F: What sport are you going to do this year, Keith?
M: I'm not sure, Judy. I'm not keen on doing football again this year. I was thinking of joining the swimming club. What do you think of that?
F: That sounds cool. Swimming is good exercise.
M: Yeah. I was also thinking about taking up athletics so that I can try doing the long jump. It's really exciting to see how far you can go.
F: I agree that athletics can be fun, but I'd still rather do team sports. So I'm signing up for the football team again. I hope I'll be captain this year. But if you prefer long jump and swimming, I say go ahead and do both.

Now listen again.
That is the end of Part One.

PART TWO
Now turn to Part Two, questions 8 to 13. You will hear a teenager called Jack Laird talking about moving to another country. For each question, choose the correct answer A, B or C.
You now have 45 seconds to look at the questions for Part 2.

Now we are ready to start. Listen carefully. You will hear the recording twice.

I'm Jack Laird, and I'm here today to tell you what it was like for me to move to a new country.
Two years ago, I moved to Spain with my family because my dad got a new job there. It might sound exciting, but the truth is, it can be quite difficult. In order to make things easier, it's really important to prepare before you go. I know, because I didn't, and it wasn't as easy as I had imagined. For example, when I got there, I couldn't understand what anyone was saying. I couldn't say anything but 'please' and 'thank you' in Spanish. I didn't even have a good dictionary. I had to have Spanish lessons before I could do anything else. I wish I'd paid attention to my Spanish teacher at school before we moved. I think that is the most important piece of advice I can give you.
It's also important to understand what the climate is like where you are going. We'd had summer holidays in Spain before, so we knew a bit about it. But when you're living there, it's hard to get used to the hot weather! The sun shines all day for six or seven months, and it never gets really cold, which is very different from where I come from in Scotland, where it's cloudy and rainy most of the time. Of course, you need to have the right kind of clothes for the type of climate, too. We'd brought all the clothes that we had with us, but I didn't have enough suitable clothes for the warm climate, so I had to buy a lot of new ones in Spain.

In any new country, you have to get used to eating different kinds of food. When we moved to Spain, the first time Mum went to the supermarket, she had a problem finding some things we used to eat. For example, in Scotland <u>we loved to eat sausages for breakfast, but</u> <u>in Spain, they didn't have my favourite ones anywhere.</u> They had different sausages, but I didn't like them much. That's one thing I miss and I really enjoy eating when I go back to visit our relatives in Scotland. When I moved to Spain, <u>I really missed my friends from home. At first, I felt too shy to try to speak to other kids in Spanish,</u> so it took me a long time to make friends. It was no fun being on my own. So if you're moving to another country, my advice is simple: <u>find out as much as you can about the country you're going to before you go there. If you learn to speak the language at least a little bit, it will be much easier to make friends when you get there.</u> Discovering a new country can really be a great adventure <u>if you're ready for it</u>!

Now listen again.
That is the end of Part Two.

PART THREE
Now turn to Part Three, questions 14 to 19. You will hear some public announcements at an airport. For each question, fill in the missing information in the numbered space.
You now have 20 seconds to look at Part 3.

Now we are ready to start. Listen carefully. You will hear the recording twice.

Good afternoon, this is the information desk. Please listen carefully to the following announcements.
We are sorry to inform passengers on United flight 930 to Edinburgh that there will be a <u>three</u>-hour delay before your flight leaves from Gate 4, due to problems with the plane's engines. We apologise for this and promise you that we are doing everything we can to fix the problem. The flight should be ready to leave at about five o'clock.
For passengers who want to change money into another currency, we remind you that the bank in Terminal B is closed for a few weeks, but the office in Terminal <u>A</u> is open.
If you get lost or separated from your group or family, please go to the meeting point in Terminal A and tell someone at the <u>information</u> desk there. Our staff will be happy to assist you, and will make an announcement for you.
There are security staff walking around the airport performing security checks, so they may stop you to ask you where you are travelling to. They may ask to see your <u>boarding pass</u>. This is for your safety and we apologise if it causes passengers any delay.
We request that passengers keep their luggage with them at all times. Please do not leave your luggage anywhere. Any <u>bags</u> found on their own will be removed by security staff.
This is an important message for passenger John MacDonald travelling to Toronto, passenger John MacDonald. Please go to <u>Passport Control</u> immediately as you have left your passport there. Please hurry as your plane cannot wait any longer and flight TE680 to Toronto is ready for take off. Passenger John MacDonald to Passport Control, please.
We apologise again to passengers waiting to travel to Edinburgh. We hope you have a pleasant time in the airport and a comfortable journey. Thank you.

Now listen again.
That is the end of Part Three.

PART FOUR
Now turn to Part Four, questions 20 to 25. Look at the six sentences for this part. You will hear a conversation between a girl, Jill, and a boy, Nick, about food. Decide if each sentence is correct or incorrect. If it is correct, choose the letter A for YES. If it is not correct, choose the letter B for NO.
You now have twenty seconds to look at the questions for Part Four.

Now we are ready to start. Listen carefully. You will hear the recording twice.

F: What shall we have to eat, Nick? I'm so hungry.
M: I don't know, Jill. Why don't we go out? <u>I wouldn't mind having something at the café</u> down the road.
F: Erm, no. Let's phone up and order something. If you've got a menu from a pizza place, we can call them and they'll deliver it. It won't take very long.
M: <u>No, I don't really feel like a pizza. I had pizza yesterday.</u>
F: Well, I suppose they are quite expensive, and we haven't got much money, anyway.
M: So maybe we could make something? There's lots of stuff in the kitchen. <u>I'm a great cook, you know.</u>
F: <u>Are you? I didn't know that.</u> What ingredients have you got in the fridge, then?
M: Let's have a look. We've got eggs, cheese and some mushrooms … and a bottle of milk.
F: Oh. What can you make with that?
M: How about a cheese and mushroom omelette?
F: Sounds tasty. <u>I've never tried to cook an omelette. I've made other things before,</u> you know, like sandwiches and salads, but not an omelette. How do you make it?
M: We need a frying pan and a little oil. I'll cut up the mushrooms and fry them a little first, and then I'll mix the eggs and put them in.
F: What's the milk for?
M: Well, <u>I can mix the milk in with the eggs to make it a bit creamier. But I don't have to if you don't want me to.</u>
F: Let's put it in. It'll be nice and creamy. What can we have for dessert? I'd love some ice cream.
M: Hey, there's some here in the freezer. Vanilla or chocolate?
F: No strawberry?
M: Sorry. No strawberry. That's your favourite, isn't it?
F: Yes. Never mind. <u>I think I'd prefer some of these grapes</u>, then.
M: Good idea. They're much healthier. Let's get started!

Now listen again.
That is the end of the test.

Practice Test 6

This is the Preliminary English Test for Schools, Practice Test 6. There are four parts to the test. You will hear each part twice.

Now open your question paper and look at Part One.

PART ONE
There are seven questions in this part. For each question there are three pictures and a short recording. For each question, choose the correct answer (A, B or C).
Before we start, here is an example.
What is the boy's favourite thing in his bedroom?

F: Oh, I love your new bedroom, Paul! Is that a new desk over there? I wish I had a big one like that.
M: Yeah, it's perfect, especially for doing my homework, but <u>the best thing about this room is the TV.</u>
F: Wow, that's amazing! I love flat-screen TVs. You're so lucky!
M: I know – it's fantastic! I've also got a new DVD player, so I just need to buy some good speakers now, and then I can have film nights in here.

The answer is C.
Look at the three pictures for question 1 now.

Now we are ready to start. Listen carefully. You will hear each recording twice.

One   Where will Tony meet his friend?
F: Hi Tony. Shall we meet at the underground station on Saturday at about three o'clock? Then we can walk down to the chess club together.
M: Well, if you know where the club is, we could just meet there.
F: That's the problem, I don't! I've never been to the chess club before. Is it near the station?
M: Not really. I know! I'll meet you outside the newsagent's on Sharp Street. It's half way between the station and the park, and it's closer to my house. See you there!

Now listen again.

Two   How will Gail get into town?
M: How are you getting into town this afternoon, Gail?
F: I'll probably get the bus. I'd get a taxi but they're just so expensive!
M: Yeah, don't waste your money. Actually, I think Mum is going to the supermarket in a little while so she'll probably give you a lift in the car. You should ask her, she's in the garden.
F: Oh, yes! I forgot she had to go out today. I'll check what time she's going, and get a lift with her, then.

Now listen again.

Three What will be on the radio tonight?
On tomorrow's show we'll be talking to Lisa Redding about her new book Dance Away, and the concerts that she'll be giving this summer. Tonight, though, we'll be asking you to pick your favourite songs of the week. So call us or text us the names of the bands and the songs that you've been listening to. Dan Pear is back on the morning show tomorrow talking about your favourite sports, so don't forget to tune in!

Now listen again.

Four   What is David going to do?
F: David, can you give me a hand with the housework, please? The house is a real mess!
M: Sure, Mum, but please don't make me do the ironing. I really hate that!
F: OK, I'll do the ironing. You can do the dishes or clean the kitchen. It's up to you. Lucy can help as well.
M: I don't mind cleaning the kitchen, but do I have to do the dishes as well? Maybe Lucy can wash them and that way we'll do it all more quickly!

Now listen again.

Five   Which is the first sports day event?
Welcome to Hill Grove School Sports Day. We have a fun day ahead! At twelve o'clock, students will be taking part in the running competition on the school playing field. Before that though, six teams will be playing against each other in the basketball tournament over on the basketball courts. While that is happening, students will be preparing for the hockey matches that will start later this morning. We hope you're ready for an exciting sports day here at Hill Grove School.

Now listen again.

Six   What is Hannah going to do at the weekend?
M: What are you going to do this weekend, Hannah?
F: Well, it's my cousin's birthday and I think she's having a party. I'm not sure I'm going to go though because it's quite far away.
M: Well, don't forget we have loads of maths homework from yesterday. You could do that at the weekend.
F: Oh, I've already done that. It didn't really take very long. To be honest, I think I'll just relax and start the book that I've bought.
M: Sounds nice.

Now listen again.

Seven Which animal does Tony's family have?
M: I saw Tony yesterday and he told me that his family got a new pet at the weekend. Guess what pet they got?
F: Well, I know his mum and his sister really wanted a cat, but his dad wanted a dog. Which one did they choose in the end?
M: Neither! They got a … snake! Can you believe it?
F: Wow, really? That's weird because I was sure they'd get a dog. I'm really surprised. It sounds cool, though!

Now listen again.
That is the end of Part One.

PART TWO
Now turn to Part Two, questions 8 to 13. You will hear part of an interview with a boy called Matt Morris, who is talking about school rules and how he feels about them. For each question, choose the correct answer A, B or C.
You now have 45 seconds to look at the questions for Part Two.

Now we are ready to start. Listen carefully. You will hear the recording twice.

F: Today we're talking to Matt Morris, sixteen, about how school rules make life easier or more difficult for students. So, Matt, tell us, what do you think about basic school rules?
M: Well, I don't agree with all of them, but generally, I think they're a good idea. I think school would be out of control if there weren't any rules like 'no running in the corridors' or 'no eating in the classroom'. When there are as many kids as there are at my school, there have to be some rules so we all know what's allowed and what isn't. Otherwise, no one would actually go to lessons or learn anything, and that's the whole reason for going to school!
F: In many schools, students might get detention if they break the rules. Detention means that students have to stay behind after school or come into school on Saturdays. What do you think about this kind of punishment?
M: To be honest, I think it's a big waste of time! Students these days have so much homework to do that they don't really have time to sit in the classroom after lessons just because their shirt is untidy or they're wearing trainers instead of school shoes. Also, I think that teachers give students detention when they don't know what else to do. I think teachers should find a better way to deal with students who cause trouble or stop other people from concentrating in class.
F: How do you feel about school uniforms, Matt? Are they a good idea, or a bad one?
M: Well, a bit of both really. The good thing is that you don't have to worry every morning about what you're going to wear to school. And it means that you don't have to think about how nice or expensive your clothes are because everyone wears the same style. I know in schools in other countries there's a lot of competition about who has the nicest or the most fashionable clothing at school. I do think uniforms are a bit boring, though. We all look the same and that means that everyone treats us the same – like a group of robots! I think that when you have to wear the same thing as hundreds of other students, you have to find a way of showing your personality.
F: What is the one thing that you would change about school, if you could?
M: Well, I'd keep the school days the same length, so we'd still get to school at half past eight and leave at three, but I'd make sure we'd have more breaks in between lessons. I think that even five or ten minutes outside the classroom can really help and I know I always concentrate better after I've had a break.

Now listen again.
That is the end of Part 2.

PART THREE

Now turn to Part Three, questions 14 to 19. You will hear a recipe for a dessert. For each question, fill in the missing information in the numbered space.
You now have 20 seconds to look at Part 3.

Now we are ready to start. Listen carefully. You will hear the recording twice.

Over the last three weeks we've been making desserts, so today we're going to show you how to make a simple but delicious chocolate cake. To start with, you have to remember to switch the oven on and let it heat up to one hundred and eighty degrees. Then weigh your ingredients and find a baking tin. Put some butter all around the edges of the tin. This stops any of the mixture sticking to the sides of the tin when you cook it.
Now we can start with the ingredients. Put one hundred and seventy-five grams of butter into a bowl. Make sure you take it out of the fridge early so that it goes a bit soft. Add a hundred and sixty-five grams of sugar and mix well. Some people like to use the same amount of sugar as butter, but I prefer to use a bit less. Even if you do like sweet desserts, make sure you don't put more than one hundred and ninety grams of sugar in. Once you've mixed that together, you can add one hundred and fifty grams of flour, fifty grams of cocoa, three large eggs and one teaspoon of baking powder. Keep stirring until it's all mixed together and there are no lumps. After twenty minutes, the oven should be hot enough, so spoon the mixture into the baking tin and put it in the oven. Make sure you check it after thirty minutes, but cook it for forty-five minutes. Open the oven door slowly so that a sudden change of temperature doesn't make the cake go flat. Be careful not to burn yourself on the oven. Wear oven gloves to handle the hot baking tin. To find out if the cake is ready, stick a fork into the middle carefully and pull it out. If it comes out clean, then it's ready. If the fork is sticky, then the cake needs to stay in the oven a bit longer.
When the cake is cooked, put on the oven gloves and take it out of the oven. Then leave the cake to cool. After it has cooled, you can melt some chocolate and cover the top of the cake with it. Wait for the chocolate to dry. Then cut the cake and serve some to your family and friends. They're sure to love it!

Now listen again.
That is the end of Part 3.

PART FOUR

Now turn to Part Four, questions 20 to 25. Look at the six sentences for this part. You will hear a conversation between a girl, Nancy, and a boy, Dan, about a friend who has a broken leg. Decide if each sentence is correct or incorrect. If it is correct, choose the letter A for YES. If it is not correct, choose the letter B for NO.
You now have 20 seconds to look at the questions for Part Four.

Now we are ready to start. Listen carefully. You will hear the recording twice.

F: Did you hear that Vicky broke her leg on Monday? She fell and hurt it badly at basketball practice.
M: Yes, I did! That must be horrible. I mean, she won't be able to play in the team for weeks.
F: That's true. But I think the worst thing is just not being able to get around as usual. Of course, she can't walk easily, but I think it makes everything else more difficult, too. Even things like having a shower or getting out of bed must be hard. The simple things, you know?
M: You're right. I can't imagine not being able to do things for myself and always asking for help. I wouldn't like to depend on anyone else.
F: At least bones get better quite quickly. I've read on the Internet that it takes about six weeks, so it's not too long.

M: Well, I'm sure it would seem longer to you if you couldn't do all the things that you usually can. Just think about it – you wouldn't be able to put on your jeans for six weeks!
F: Yeah, having a broken leg must be a terrible experience. Poor Vicky!
M: I would prefer to have a broken arm than a broken leg. That way I could still go out with my friends, but I wouldn't have to do my homework!
F: Well, when you say it like that, it doesn't sound so serious, but it would probably hurt just as much as a broken leg. My cousin broke her arm and she said it was very painful. I think breaking any bone is horrible!
M: It must really hurt, especially when it's just happened. And it would be so annoying if you had to go back to the hospital every week to have it checked.
F: You know what? I think we should go and see Vicky. She must feel so bad about being stuck at home all the time. Let's go and keep her company.
M: That's a good idea. We can take her some magazines to make her feel better.

Now listen again.
That is the end of the test.

Practice Test 7

This is the Preliminary English Test for Schools, Practice Test 7. There are four parts to the test. You will hear each part twice.

Now open your question paper and look at Part One.

PART ONE

There are seven questions in this part. For each question, there are three pictures and a short recording. For each question, choose the correct answer, (A, B or C).
Before we start, here is an example.
What are they going to do?

M: Hey, what's wrong? You look a bit worried.
F: Oh, I'm late and I'm going to miss the bus and there isn't another one for half an hour. I'm going to be so late for volleyball practice!
M: Come on, I'll help you. What do you need to do before you go?
F: I have to find my keys, but they seem to have disappeared!
M: Take it easy! I'll help you look for them. Now, where did you last see them?

The answer is A.
Look at the three pictures for question 1 now.

Now we are ready to start. Listen carefully. You will hear each recording twice.

One   What present is the girl going to give her friend?
F1:   Hi! Can I help you?
F2:   Yes, please. I'm looking for a present for my best friend. It's her birthday tomorrow. I like those earrings. How much are they?
F1:   Oh, they're twenty-five euros.
F2:   Hmm, they're a bit expensive. What about that belt over there?
F1:   This one? It's twelve euros.
F2:   Right. I'm sure that'll look good with her new jeans. Could you gift-wrap it for me, please?

Now listen again.

Two   What will the weather be like today?
And now the weather forecast. First, some good news for all of us. After all the foggy and wet weather we've had this week, the weather will be much brighter from tomorrow.

The temperature will rise and the weather will be warm and sunny in most parts of the country. However, you still need to be a bit patient because for today the temperature is going to remain low and it's going to be cloudy with quite a bit of wind in most parts of the country.

Now listen again.

Three Where was Janet last night?
F: Hey, Donald! Wait for me! What's the hurry?
M: Hi, Janet. Sorry, I'm late for the dentist. I didn't see you at the youth club last night – where were you?
F: Well, you know that I like singing. So yesterday I went to an audition – they're looking for singers for that new TV show, so I went to give it a try! But what's wrong with you? Have you got a toothache?
M: No, nothing like that. I'm just going to have my teeth checked. Hey! So are you ready to become a big star, then?

Now listen again.

Four Which programme will be on before the news?
Here are some changes to this evening's programmes. Due to the weather conditions, today's live tennis match has been cancelled and in its place there will be a documentary about ocean life and global warming – that's at quarter past six. That will be followed by the news at half past seven. The science fiction adventure series, Alien Planet, instead of starting at seven o'clock, will begin at quarter past eight, just after the news.

Now listen again.

Five What do the students have to do at the art gallery?
Now, listen carefully, please. When we arrive at the gallery, you'll be working in pairs. You need to find information about the painters and their paintings and then write it in your project notes. You may go into any room in the gallery, but you must NOT leave the building at any time. If you want to buy a snack or a drink, there's a café in the basement. When it's time to leave at half past one, please meet in front of the gallery ticket desk. Any questions? All right, let's go.

Now listen again.

Six What does the boy order?
F: Hi! What can I get you?
M: Hello. Erm … can I have a look at the menu, please?
F: Certainly, here you are.
M: Hmm … right, well I think I'll have the small vegetarian pizza and a salad and …
F: I'm afraid we've just run out of vegetarian pizza. Would you like to choose something else?
M: Oh, OK. I'll have the spaghetti with tomato sauce, a salad and … let me see … an orange juice to drink, please.

Now listen again.

Seven What has Philip forgotten to take with him?
Hi, Mum. It's Philip here. We've just arrived at the camp, but I've got a problem. I think I left some things at home. Can you see if my MP3 player is on my bed? I can't find it in my bag. Oh, no, sorry, here it is. Well, I still can't find my camera and my toothbrush. Are they there? Perhaps I left the camera on my desk. Oh, don't look for the toothbrush – I've just discovered it together with the toothpaste. Call me when you find the camera, will you, Mum? Thanks, bye!

Now listen again.
That is the end of Part One.

PART TWO
Now turn to Part Two, questions, 8 to 13. You will hear an advertisement for a health club. For each question, choose the correct answer, (A, B or C).
You now have 45 seconds to look at the questions for Part 2.

Now we are ready to start. Listen carefully. You will hear the recording twice.

Do you feel the need to build up your strength and add a few pounds of muscle? Are you getting worried that your clothes don't fit any more because you've put on too much weight? Or maybe you simply want to look and feel your best this summer. Whatever your situation, there's a new health club in town just for you! At Love Your Body, you'll find what you've been looking for. We have special programmes for teenagers, with our expert personal trainers to encourage you and give you advice.
And with a huge swimming pool, an indoor track, and volleyball, basketball, tennis and squash courts, our health club is the ideal place for teenagers to exercise and get in shape while having fun with their friends. And there'll be no mums and dads in sight, because every evening from 5 to 7 it's teenagers only! We have a great gym with modern equipment where we also offer Pilates classes, as well as Power Yoga and Zumba, the new craze! Don't know what that is? Come and try a session, and if you don't immediately fall in love with this combination of dance, aerobics and fantastic Latin music, then you can have your money back!
And that's not all we have to offer: there's a café where you can enjoy fresh fruit juices or healthy snacks after your workout, and there's a shop where you can buy sports equipment and clothes, and also books on dieting and healthy eating habits. You can also find sport and fitness magazines from around the world.
And I've kept the best for last! Love Your Body isn't expensive at all! We've kept the membership fee down especially because we want younger people to be able to afford it. We know you don't get much pocket money, and your parents haven't got a lot of spare cash either. So, here's the offer: if you sign up for six months or more, you get a discount of fifty per cent! Yes, that's right! Fifty per cent off if you decide to join the club for six months or more. And for those of you who haven't made up your minds yet, here's another offer: come for a month at the standard price of fifteen pounds a month. Then, if you decide to stay on, get the same fifty per cent discount for the next six months. For more details, contact us at info@loveyourbody.co.uk.

Now listen again.
That is the end of Part Two.

PART THREE
Now turn to Part Three, questions 14 to 19. You will hear some information about a history museum and an exhibition. For each question, fill in the missing information in the numbered space.
You now have 20 seconds to look at Part Three.

Now we are ready to start. Listen carefully. You will hear the recording twice.

Good afternoon, children, and welcome to our museum. I hope you'll enjoy the tour. The museum was built in 1880 but it didn't open to visitors until a year later. Now, it's got amazing collections of artwork, writing, jewellery and more from all over the world.
As we go through the entrance to the hall on your right, you can see a map of the Ancient Worlds. This shows dates and facts about every country in our Ancient Worlds exhibition. There are also more general leaflets about the museum and opening and closing times.
As you walk into the first hall, you can't miss our main feature. This collection from ancient Egypt includes some of the most exciting objects found over the years. Our smaller Greek and Roman collections are at the back of this hall and

they make up this month's Ancient Worlds display. Please stay together as a class while we take a good look at the exhibits. And please don't touch anything in here because some things may break very easily. You'll be able to play with the working models in our interactive section later.

The large case in front of you contains a model of King Tutankhamun, the most famous of all Egyptian kings. Tutankhamun was only a <u>nine</u>-year-old boy when he became king. He died at the age of nineteen and was buried in a special room, known as a tomb, along with his money and treasure.

For many years even Egyptian archaeologists didn't know there was a tomb, that is, until it was discovered by <u>English</u> archaeologist Howard Carter in 1922. The discovery caused a lot of excitement all over the world, and since then people have become more and more interested in ancient Egypt.

The display cabinet over there on the right contains just some of the things from the tomb. You'll see jewellery, special sweet smelling oils and a copy of Tutankhamun's <u>mask</u>: an image that Egypt has become famous for.

Now listen again.
That is the end of Part 3.

PART FOUR
Now turn to Part Four, questions 20 to 25. Look at the six sentences for this part. You will hear a conversation between a girl, Celia, and a boy, Ryan, about a personal problem that Ryan has. Decide if each sentence is correct or incorrect. If it is correct, choose the letter A for YES. If it is not correct, choose the letter B for NO.
You now have twenty seconds to look at the questions for Part 4.

Now we are ready to start. Listen carefully. You will hear the recording twice.

F: Hi, Ryan. <u>What's up? You seem a bit upset. Has something happened?</u>
M: Oh, hi, Celia. Well, yes, something has happened, actually.
F: Oh? What's wrong? Did anything happen at home, or at school maybe?
M: No, nothing like that, but you see … do you remember that I <u>wanted a new mobile phone? A smartphone – one with a touch screen and everything</u>? A phone that would connect on the Internet and I'd be able to download music and get into my profile and things?
F: Yes, I remember. <u>But your parents said 'no' every time you asked them,</u> didn't they?
M: Yes, they did. Then, last month, when it was my birthday, I asked them again. This time they agreed to get me one as a present <u>if I paid half the money.</u>
F: That's great! So, did you manage to find the money? What happened?
M: Yes, I did. That's the trouble …
F: Trouble? I don't understand. You should be happy about it.
M: I got the phone and I was so happy with it! Really excited! It was everything I wanted. Yesterday, <u>I took it to school and showed it to my best friend.</u>
F: Uh-oh! I have a bad feeling about this.
M: You're right of course. You know we aren't allowed to have mobile phones at school, don't you? Well, a teacher saw me playing with it …
F: Oh dear! So what did she do?
M: She took my new phone and said I can have it back at the end of the school year! The end of the school year! That's five months away! What am I going to do? How shall I explain that to my parents? I promised them that I wouldn't take the phone to school. Now what?
F: Yes, you're in trouble. Poor Ryan! Have you tried talking to the teacher? If you explained to her and promised never to bring it back to school, perhaps she might give it back.

M: Yes, I'll do that tomorrow. But if she refuses to give it back to me, <u>I'll have to tell my parents – they're going to be so angry!</u> I don't think they'll ever buy me a single thing again.

Now listen again.
That is the end of the test.

Practice Test 8

This is the Preliminary English Test for Schools, Practice Test 8. There are four parts to the test. You will hear each part twice.

Now open your question paper and look at Part One.

PART ONE
There are seven questions in this part. For each question, there are three pictures and a short recording. For each question, choose the correct answer (A, B or C).
Before we start, here is an example.
What is the girl going to have?

F: Hi! <u>I'd like a sandwich, please. The one with tomato and lettuce.</u>
M: Sure. Would you like anything to drink?
F: Erm, I'm not fond of cola, so could I have an orange juice, please?
M: There isn't any orange juice, but there's a pineapple and banana mix. Do you fancy that?
F: Hmm … not really. <u>Just water will be fine, then.</u>
M: No problem. Here you go. That'll be two pounds fifty, please.

The answer is B.
Look at the three pictures for question 1 now.

Now we are ready to start. Listen carefully. You will hear each recording twice.

One   What is the girl going to take to the park?
F: What a beautiful sunny day! Why don't we go out? Shall we go to the park?
M: Good idea! I'll get my MP3 player to listen to some music. I've got Justin's new album!
F: OK, <u>I'll take this with me: my favourite science-fiction book!</u>
M: Weren't you reading that at school? I thought you'd finished it already!
F: Nearly! I'm in the middle of the last chapter! It's so good!
M: I know. That's where the spaceship captain discovers the truth! Come on! Let's go!

Now listen again.

Two   What did the singer like most?
F: James, you've just finished your European tour. Tell us about it!
M: Well, my fans here in Europe are wonderful – but <u>what I enjoyed most about this tour was my new team; they're fantastic. I had a great time with them during the concert and after it!</u>
F: And you must have enjoyed staying in the most famous hotel in London!
M: Yes, it was beautiful, but I'm used to staying in big hotels.
F: Thanks, James. Good luck with your new album!

Now listen again.

Three   When will they go on holiday?
F: I really want to go to Cuba this year. Shall we go in August?

M: I suppose I could take a week off. But they say it's really hot between June and August. Why don't we go in December?
F: We could … but wait! Your sister's coming over from Australia then, remember?
M: Yes, you're right. How could I forget that? So we can't go in December. I say we leave it till next year, in spring. Maybe in April or May.
F: Promise?
M: Yes, I promise!

Now listen again.

Four   What exam does the teacher announce for Friday?
Sit down and be quiet, please. I've got the exam results from Monday here. You've all passed the maths test, but you didn't do as well in physics. I'll give you your marks on Friday after your geography exam. This last one will be on European rivers and mountains. Remember to hand in your projects on historical battles on Thursday. You know this is a busy week, so plan your study time – don't waste it!

Now listen again.

Five   What time is it now?
M: Mum! What time are you picking me up today?
F: The same time I always pick you up. Why?
M: Well, I've got football practice today and I can't be late!
F: Don't worry! You'll make it in time! But hurry up now! It's five past already! You'll miss the bus!
M: The bus comes at half past eight. I still have twenty-five minutes!
F: Well, come on! You're still in your pyjamas! You know it takes you ages to get ready!
M: All right …

Now listen again.

Six   What is the girl drinking?
M: Don't drink that now! We're going to have lunch in a minute!
F: I've nearly finished it, Dad.
M: You shouldn't have anything sweet before lunch! Now you're not hungry and you won't eat your lunch.
F: It's not sweet, Dad! It's not like cola! It says it's 100% pineapple and there's no sugar in it. Anyway, weren't you drinking a cup of tea five minutes ago?
M: I was, but that's different! Come on! Your mum's calling.
F: Don't worry, Dad! I'll leave a clean plate, you'll see!

Now listen again.

Seven Who is going to take the dog for a walk?
F1: Mary, could you take Max for a walk? He's been inside all day. He needs a bit of fresh air.
F2: Oh, Mum, I can't. I'm riding my bicycle to the park. Why can't Dad take him? A little bit of walking would do him good.
F1: He's not here. He's coming home late today. And your brother is upstairs; he's not feeling very well.
F2: Oh, all right, Mum. I'll walk to the park, then.
F1: Thanks, Mary. Don't be late for lunch, please!
F2: I won't!

Now listen again.
That is the end of Part One.

PART TWO
Now turn to Part Two, questions 8 to 13. You will hear part of an interview with Stacey Peterson, a young designer who makes theatre costumes. For each question, choose the correct answer A, B or C.
You now have 45 seconds to look at the questions for Part Two.

Now we are ready to start. Listen carefully. You will hear the recording twice.

M: Stacey Peterson is a costume designer. She's only 25 years old but she has been working in the theatre for years. How did it all start, Stacey?
F: When I was at university I used to live with Mary, a good friend of mine. She worked as an actress and one day she gave me a ticket to see her play at the theatre. That was my lucky day because I met her director. She loved the coat I was wearing and when I told her I had designed and made it, she offered me a job!
M: And what do you enjoy most about making theatre costumes?
F: It's hard to say really. I like to see the actors perform the play for the first time in my costumes. I must admit I get a little nervous in the beginning, especially when it's a famous play, because I'm not sure whether the audience will like the costumes. But what I really like is working in different teams in each play. People are always friendly and very creative!
M: Is it a difficult job?
F: Some designers think it's very stressful. For instance, for our next play we have to create thirty costumes in just one month. I'm very organised, so I'm the only one in our team who doesn't feel stressed! But I am going to use recycled leather for the first time and that worries me a bit.
M: And what about inspiration? Where do get your ideas from?
F: There are a lot of fashion shows here in London and I wish I had time to go and see them – but I don't. In the early days I used to go to the library and borrow books on fashion, but these days I spend a lot of time researching photos online.
M: What plans have you got for the future?
F: I would like to go back to university and do another degree – maybe something to do with film directing. But I probably won't. Studying and working at the same time is very hard. I'll keep working, but I might stop making clothes for a while. I'd love to design and make hats and shoes.
M: And what should our teenage listeners do if they want to be like you in the future?
F: Well, it's not necessary to know a lot about theatre. I mean, if they like seeing plays, that's fine, but they will learn a lot about it when they start working. It's more important to do a degree in fashion at a good university and do different creative courses such as photography and drawing.
M: It's been a pleasure talking to you, Stacey. Thank you for being with us today.
F: Thank you.

Now listen again.
That is the end of Part 2.

PART THREE
Now turn to Part Three, questions 14 to 19. You will hear some advice on how to decorate your bedroom. For each question, fill in the missing information in the numbered space.
You now have 20 seconds to look at Part Three.

Now we are ready to start. Listen carefully. You will hear the recording twice.

Is your room still painted in those kids' colours your parents chose? Do you still have shelves full of teddy bears and toys? Then maybe it's time to redecorate your bedroom. First of all, you should clean up the place and put things that you don't need any more into boxes. Don't be afraid to throw away your old toys, although it's better to give them to a charity shop. But don't throw out any furniture without asking your parents first. When you finish cleaning up, push all your furniture to the middle of your room. This will help you to imagine how much space there is and what different positions you could put things in. Draw a plan of where you would like each piece of furniture to go.

Then decide what the best style for you is. You could have an environmental theme or a sporty one – whatever you like. It could even be a rock or pop music room! It doesn't matter what style you choose – the important thing is that you focus on one main style.

Now it's time to start decorating. Keep your room personal and comfortable. If you can't buy new furniture, then be creative with what you have. Paint your desk a different colour, put your shelves on a different wall and put up some new posters. If your parents can afford to buy new sheets for your bed and new curtains, make sure you let them know what colours you prefer. And when it comes to painting your bedroom, be careful to choose the right colour. If it's too bright, it might give you a headache – and colours that are too dark could be depressing. Soft colours are the best for teenage bedrooms. They will help you relax after a long day. Many designers also recommend having a small sofa or a big armchair in the bedroom. A cheaper idea is to put a couple of big cushions on the floor. Put them in one of the corners, where you can sit and read a book or listen to music. Now, if you'd like more tips on how to decorate your bedroom, go online and check out our website.

Now listen again.
That is the end of Part 3.

PART FOUR

Now turn to Part Four, questions 20 to 25. Look at the six sentences for this part. You will hear a conversation between a brother, Andy, and sister, Carol, about the weekend. Decide if each sentence is correct or incorrect. If it is correct, choose the letter A for YES. If it is not correct, choose the letter B for NO.

You now have 20 seconds to look at the questions for Part Four.

Now we are ready to start. Listen carefully. You will hear the recording twice.

F: Hi, Andy. Why are you studying? Today's Saturday and we've just finished our exams.
M: I know your class has finished, but we haven't. Our teacher was off ill yesterday, so we're having our history exam on Monday instead. I'm going to revise a bit, that's all.
F: I can give you some help if you think you need it. It'll probably be the same as the exam I had last year. Oh, but before I forget, could I use your MP3 player? I want to listen to some music and my laptop is charging.
M: Of course, it's in my bag. No problem with history, really – I actually find it interesting this year. But thanks for offering to help, anyway.
F: What are you doing tonight? I'm going with Matt and Gill to see Dark Forest at the cinema. Do you want to come?
M: No, thanks. It's a great film, but I've seen it already. I went last Friday with Charlie. I think I'll stay in tonight. My room needs cleaning, too.
F: Yes, I heard Mum yelling at you about that! You know, we ought to help her a bit more here; she seems really tired these days. She's been working so hard at the office.
M: You're right.
F: Why don't we clean the house together tomorrow? That would be a nice surprise for her. I'll help you with your bedroom if you like.
M: Good idea! We can start early before Mum gets up for breakfast. How about making a nice Sunday lunch as well? I can make Mum's favourite – roast chicken.
F: OK. And I'll make a special salad. We've got tomatoes, cucumber and onions. I'll go to the supermarket and buy some red and green peppers.
M: Great! I'm sure she'll love it.

Now listen again.
That is the end of the test.

www.ingramcontent.com/pod-product-compliance
Ingram Content Group UK Ltd.
Pitfield, Milton Keynes, MK11 3LW, UK
UKHW052202270225
455668UK00006B/19